A Citizen-Soldier Remembers
1942-1946

A Citizen-Soldier Remembers
1942-1946

George E. McAvoy
Technician Fourth Grade

**149th Armored Signal Company
of the
9th Armored Division**

The Crawford Press
Littleton, New Hampshire
1991

The author makes grateful acknowledgment to David Hutchings for permission to use portions of his book, *R.M.S. Queen Mary, 50 Years of Splendour*.

Crawford Press
Box 235
Littleton, NH 03561

Produced by Peter E. Randall Publisher
Box 4726, Portsmouth, NH 03802-4726
Design by Tom Allen

ISBN 0-9630647-2-X

TO MY MOTHER

When my father was killed in 1920, she was left with three very young children. I was three months old. She dedicated her life to raising her three boys, and when we all went into the service during World War II, she kept a scrapbook covering anything written about her sons or the units with which they served. Although she is now gone many years, this book could not have been written if she had not saved much of this information.

Books by George E. McAvoy

And Then There Was One
A 200-year-plus history covering the area from the top of Mount Washington, New Hampshire, and the west side of the mountain. This history also discusses the development of the North Country and the great hotels in the town of Carroll, New Hampshire. There are fifty color pictures and more than 100 black-and-white pictures. This book sells for $37.95, including shipping and handling (Crawford Press, Box 235, Littleton, NH 03561).

The Inn Thing
This satiric story covers the true experiences of the author and his family in the hotel business over many years. It begins with a couple checking into a hotel and expressing interest in being in the hospitality industry. Each employee of the hotel discusses with the couple his or her personal experience in the business. The book takes the couple through each staff position, including a consultant and a club manager. It begins with a doorman and then moves to the bellboy, desk clerk, chambermaid, etc. Anyone in the hospitality industry will find this book intriguing and will find it easy to relate to the many true stories. (This manuscript is still in progress.)

Contents

Acknowledgments

Phantom Nine, by Dr. Walter E. Reichelt

The Bridge, printed in Bayreuth, Germany, by Carl Giessel

The 9th: The Story of the 9th Armored Division, issued by the
    Orientation Branch, Information and Education Services, HQ, TSFET

Stars and Stripes

Manchester Union Leader

Queen Mary, Commemorative Pictorial, Wrather Corporation, by Rosebud
    Books

RMS Queen Mary, 50 Years of Splendour, by David F. Hutchings

The Golden Age of Transatlantic Travel, 1936-1959, by Jane Hunter-Cox

Supreme Headquarters, Press Release, January 4, 1945

New York World Telegram

Toledo Times, Acme Photo

General Orders #81, 9th Armored Division, May 9, 1945

Meritorious Unit Citation, 9th Armored Division

War Department Pamphlet #21-31: Two Down and One to Go

Certificate, Captured Enemy Equipment, Headquarters, United States
    Forces, European Theater

Bill Winberg, Historian, Queen Mary and Spruce Goose

The White House

U.S. Army Center of Military History

Personal photos and records of George E. McAvoy

Columbia Viking Desk Encyclopedia

A Short Guide to Great Britain. War and Navy Departments, Washington,
    D.C.

Queen Mary Historical Archives

Imperial War Museum

Steamship Historical Society of America

Wide World Photos, Inc.

Central Press Photos, Ltd.

Norman Sivin, Bethlehem, NH

Introduction

World War II, 1939-1945

The Columbia Viking Desk Encyclopedia (1953 edition) contains a succinct and very useful summary of the second Great War of the twentieth century; the information below is adapted from it.

The chief political events leading to World War II were the aggressive policies of the principal Axis powers — Germany, Italy, and Japan — culminating in the German seizure of Bohemia and Moravia (March 1939). The Western powers — Great Britain and France — after crowning their "appeasement policy" with the Munich Pact in 1938, began to rearm, and they extended guarantees to other possible victims of aggression, notably Poland. While Adolf Hitler demanded the return of Danzig and the Polish Corridor, the USSR concluded a nonaggression pact with Germany (August 1939). Hitler thus was left free to break off negotiations and attack Poland (September 1). Great Britain (joined by nearly all the members of the British Commonwealth) and France declared war on Germany. German lightning tactics (Blitzkrieg) won a quick victory in Poland.

In the West, the British and French spent an inactive winter behind the Maginot Line. In April 1940, Germany invaded and occupied Denmark and Norway. In May, it overran the Low Countries, broke into France, swept to France's English Channel ports, and cut off the allies, who were evacuated from Dunkirk. Italy entered the war on June 10, 1940. On June 22, France surrendered. Britain, under Winston Churchill's leadership, fought on alone. In the Battle of Britain, the United Kingdom resisted Germany's attempt to bomb it into submission. Land operations continued in North Africa, where Italy attacked the British, and in the Balkans, where Italy attacked Greece (October 1940) and where Germany, Hungary, and Bulgaria invaded Yugoslavia (April 1941).

The first round appeared to have been won by the axis, and on June 22, 1941, Hitler launched an invasion of the USSR. Meanwhile, the United States was gradually drawn closer to war. Congress voted lend-lease aid to Britain (1941), and, to protect its shipping, the United States occupied Iceland and Greenland.

Japanese aggression in Indochina and Thailand led to extreme

Manchester Union headline, December 8, 1941.

tension, and then, on December 7, 1941, Japan attacked Pearl Harbor, the Philippines, and Malaya. The United States — followed by most of the allies (except the USSR) — declared war on Japan. Germany and its allies (except Finland) declared war on the United States. By 1942, Japan had conquered the Philippines, many other Pacific islands, and all of Southeast Asia; in the Soviet Union, the axis forces had reached Stalingrad and the Caucasus; in Africa, General Rommel seemed about to take Cairo; in naval warfare, German submarines threatened to wipe out allied shipping. At this dark hour, the allies rallied and turned the tide in a series of victories. In North Africa, General Montgomery's victory at El Alamein (October 1942) — followed by the U.S. landing in Algeria — resulted in total victory over the axis forces, the allied conquest of Sicily and southern Italy, and Italy's surrender (September 1943). In the Pacific, the United States won the naval battles of Coral Sea and Midway, landed at Guadalcanal (1942), and, under the leadership of General Douglas MacArthur and Admirals William Halsey and Chester Nimitz, began the "island-hopping" strategy that by 1945 had won back the Philippines and brought a strike force to Japan's doorstep at Iwo Jima and Okinawa. In the USSR, the victory of Stalingrad (1943) was followed by the mighty Soviet drive that by 1944 brought Russian armies deep into Poland and Hungary and drove the axis powers out of the Balkans.

The "Battle of the Atlantic" ended with the virtual extermination of German submarines. In central Italy, the allies met stubborn German resistance that required slow, grueling warfare, but on June 6, 1944, the allies, under the command of General Dwight Eisenhower, landed in Normandy. In August, a second allied force landed in southern France. By late 1944, France and Belgium were liberated and the war was carried into the Netherlands and Germany. Allied air power was annihilating Germany's industrial centers.

* * *

Much has been written about World War II, and this book is not an effort to change anything that has already been published, but rather to provide the perspective of an eyewitness to some of the historic — and not so historic — events.

The first peacetime conscription in U.S. history was undertaken in 1940, giving the United States a little more than one year to start training an armed force of navy, army, marines, coast guard, and air force. This also spurred the wheels of industry to produce the necessary supplies.

The training of approximately 8.5 million military personnel to create a combat team that would face the mighty Nazi war machine and the Japanese forces in the Pacific was a mammoth undertaking. The whole alteration of our peacetime economy into a massive military buildup was just as mammoth an undertaking. This book covers the European Theater of Operations, and only the part where I was involved. I have addressed the subject from my own point of view.

It begins with my enlistment in the service and continues with tornadoes in Kansas, sandstorms in the Mojave Desert of California, the training of both officers and men during these periods, war-game exercises at Camp Polk in Louisiana, and finally the orders to ship out and go overseas.

Then there is the story of the 9th Armored Division being shipped overseas on the historic luxury liner Queen Mary. We proceeded to Scotland and then England, where we drew equipment and ammunition before crossing the English Channel in LSTs, landing at Omaha Beach in Normandy. Next came a triumphal eight-day trip across France to take up positions in Luxembourg. The narrative continues with the gradual introduction of the division into battle, culminating in the Battle of the Bulge (the Ardennes) on December 16, 1944. Our 9th Armored Division found itself in the center of major fighting in three sectors.

After the Battle of the Bulge, we drew new equipment and replacements and then wintered along the Moselle River near Metz. Finally, we received orders to move to Liège, Belgium, and then strike across the Roer Valley toward the Rhine River, locale of the sensational — and well documented — capture of the Remagen railroad bridge.

The tale continues with the breakout from the bridgehead at Remagen and the events leading up to the encirclement of the German Rhine forces, followed by the dash toward Leipzig, which cut Germany in two. The story carries on with the eventual surrender of the Germans in Czechoslovakia and Austria, the restoration of German cities by German prisoners of war, the American supervision of this work, and the withdrawal of American troops from areas that were turned over to the Russians. The 9th Armored Division — only three years old when the war ended — gradually was broken up when we all returned home.

These highlights and the accompanying photographs record a very small segment of a period that is part of the glorious history of America.

Camp Funston, Fort Riley, Kansas.

One

Fort Riley, Kansas

On December 1, 1942, I enlisted in the United States Army in Lewiston, Maine, and was sent to Fort Devens, Massachusetts. Here I was issued army dress — including a heavy winter coat — and with hundreds of others boarded a troop train headed for Fort Riley, Kansas. Every piece of railroad equipment that was operational, in any way, was called back into service by the railroads, and the passenger car in which I rode was incredibly drafty. Obviously, we had landed in one of the oldest cars. We all sat huddled in our overcoats, trying to stay warm. I was very appreciative of the people in Muncie, Indiana, who had coffee and doughnuts for us in the wee hours of the morning when we made a short stop during that trip.

We arrived at Fort Riley and were assigned to the Camp Funston section. Fort Riley is a permanent army camp, but the Camp Funston section was built just to house the additional troops brought in because of the war. It was the typical two-story wooden barracks that remains in use today in some areas. We were informed that we were the final troops to round out a division that was to be known as the 9th Armored Division, a descendant of the 2nd Cavalry. (The old army group always called it the "calvary.") I was assigned to the 2nd Armored Signal Company — later renamed the 149th Armored Signal Company — and went through a series of aptitude tests to find out what I was best suited to do. Soon I was informed I would become a Morse code radio operator, and instructors began training a group of us on how to receive and send Morse code. This was done on simulated sending and receiving equipment, and we also learned the "Q signals" that stood for the short sentences most commonly used with Morse code. It wasn't long before we were fairly proficient in handling the code.

While I attended my courses, some of the other fellows were assigned to be drivers and were being taught how to drive. Unfortunately, my assignment as a radio operator precluded me from this training. Not many of us knew how to drive at that time, as automobiles were not as plentiful as they are today. Since a tank division had more than 3,000 vehicles, there had to be quite a few drivers.

The 9th Armored Division consisted, after many changes, of 10,000

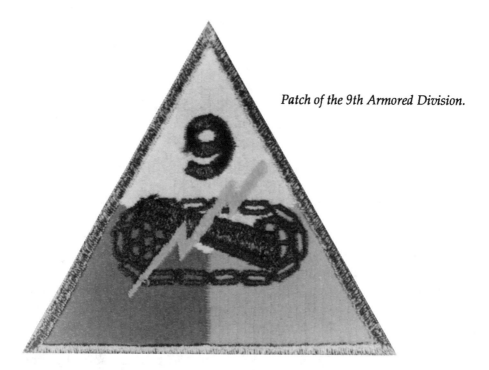

Patch of the 9th Armored Division.

men and 600 officers. Originally the division had about 15,000 men, but gradually it was streamlined and divided into three combat commands known as CCA, CCB, and CCR. Each of these commands consisted of an armored infantry battalion, a tank battalion, a self-propelled armored field artillery battalion, and support units such as engineers, medics, signal, quartermaster, etc. As the situation warranted, other units would supplement the basic grouping.

The Armored Division's patch was designed with the three main elements in color — blue for infantry, red for field artillery, and yellow for cavalry or tanks. A track in the middle of the patch was for mobility, a cannon for firepower, and a streak of lightning for shock action. The division number was in the upper corner.

The signal company's mission was to coordinate communications within the division and with corps and army by telephone, radio (both voice and Morse code), and messenger service. Telephone duty included stringing wire and maintaining that wire service.

The old army group of the 2nd Cavalry made up the cadre to form the division. These men — mostly the noncommissioned officers — knew the soldier's handbook from cover to cover. They knew what a soldier should do and what he shouldn't do and how to avoid, legally, many of the pitfalls brought about by orders from officers. At this time, the United

The ever-handy mops. Morone with mop, McAvoy back-to.

States was throwing together an armed force that would consist of more than eight million officers and men trained under a crash program. It was inevitable that some of the officers, chosen for their college degrees and for their intelligence or leadership positions in industry, would prove to be totally inept in the military. The maneuvers and training would bring out the failings in many of the newly created officers and the men under their command.

Naturally, cleanliness was one of the major concerns of the army, and every Saturday our barracks was to be mopped clean and beds were to be immaculate, after which we would stand inspection. One particular Saturday, the barracks was immaculate but the inspecting officer found a small piece of soap under one of the cots. He raised hell with the master sergeant and severely penalized the whole barracks with cancellation of weekend passes, and so on. The sergeant agreed with the lieutenant and then suggested to the lieutenant that we use lye on the floor in order to make it absolutely white. The lieutenant considered this and finally decided that it would not be necessary. The sergeant again suggested it, but the lieutenant said no. After the officer left, the sergeant said, "If he had only given me the order to do it, we would have used enough lye to eat this barracks to the ground."

In another case, one of the men had done something that infuriated the commanding officer, and he wanted the man court-martialed. The first sergeant tried to talk the CO out of a court-martial, but the CO was adamant. The soldier was confined to barracks. So the sergeant went to the CO and said, "Are we just going to let him lie around the barracks or can I put him on detail?" The CO authorized work details and the sergeant gave the man a list of the dirtiest duties a soldier could draw. The sergeant remarked that when this was all over, the man would really owe him one. At that point, we didn't know what he was talking about, but when it came time for the court-martial, the confined man claimed that he already had been punished, so he was released. The sergeant was right — the fellow did owe him one.

During training, the Articles of War were mentioned many times — primarily in reference to the fact that, if captured, all that was necessary to provide was name, rank, and serial number — no other information was to be given. In the soldier's handbook, it says that the Articles of War will be discussed from time to time. However, I don't remember any discussion except the one about name, rank, and serial number. In fact, I honestly thought that that was all there was to the Articles of War.

There were many shortages during the war, and one of them was a lack of boots — there weren't even enough to go around. And even though I came from the Northeast, I really suffered from the cold in Kansas. When the wind blows up from the south, it is warm and balmy, but the wind can suddenly change direction and blow from the north, and then the temperature plunges quickly to near zero. With all of the hikes and outdoor training, it didn't take long for me to come down with a severe case of bronchitis. I was sent to the hospital and assigned to a ward.

The following morning, as the doctor entered the ward, all of the patients were called to attention. They jumped out of bed and stood waiting for the doctor to look at them. I felt absolutely miserable, and I was not about to jump out of bed and stand at attention. This, of course, was the perfect way to get immediate attention. The doctor walked down to my bed and asked what was wrong with me. I thought that I had come there for him to tell me what was wrong. He did check me out and prescribed medicine, and before long I was feeling pretty good, but I thought that they would never release me from that place. When I finally got out, there were specific orders that I was not to participate in outdoor activities until they were able to equip me with boots.

Christmas in December of 1942 was the first of four that I would spend in the service, and all four would be under extremely different circumstances. The first was spent with the strangers I was just beginning to know in Camp Funston. Though the army scheduled plenty of entertainment during this period, it was a lonely holiday away from home.

Taking a group of men who ran the gamut of physical conditions and bringing them all up to top shape produced a lot of griping and plain old army bitching. We ran everywhere we went. We were taken through all of the obstacle courses, which included climbing walls, hand over hand on a rope across a creek, crawling through culverts, and experiencing live ammunition firing overhead while crawling through the infiltration course. We were also given compasses and ordered to travel for ten miles by compass, in full field equipment, without coming out into the open. We did this on the buddy system, and two of us made it the ten miles and came out a hundred yards from the designated target area. That accomplishment made us feel pretty proud.

We were also given the old army routine of KP duty — cleaning the pots and pans and mopping the kitchen floor. Since we all had mess kits and washed our own kits, dishwashing wasn't part of the duty. Having been in the hotel business before the army, I didn't find KP duty very appealing. We also drew our share of guard duty around the post, mostly at night. My promotion to Technician fifth grade (corporal) fortunately eliminated the KP duty.

We were on a constant training schedule that began with short hikes and brought us all the way up to a forced march of twenty-five miles in full field equipment. The day we made that march, we finished in about five and a half hours, so we immediately showered and dressed and went to town for the rest of the day. It was on one of these trips into Junction City that I met an old man in a flower shop. He was in his nineties and delighted in telling us stories of Wild Bill Hickok. The old fellow had lived in Junction City all of his life, and he remembered how Junction City had been during the Wild West. He was quite an attraction for all of the GIs in those days.

It was at Camp Funston that I learned to fire the .45-caliber army automatic, the .45-caliber Thompson submachine gun, and the .30-caliber carbine. As a boy, I had attended a military camp — Lake Delaware Boys Camp at Delhi, New York — and had learned to fire the .30-caliber 1903 Springfield rifle there. It wasn't until later in our training that we fired the machine guns. We also had a training session on the bazooka. The army always had a cute way of training a soldier how to fire a weapon. It started with taking the weapon apart and putting it back together again, and it had to be cleaned each time. We wore out those weapons cleaning them, and finally we fired them. After firing them, we were tested time and again on how clean the weapon was. You can get awful sick of

Take the machine gun apart, clean it, put it back together. Left to right: S/Sgt. Denny, S/Sgt Gates (facing camera), T/5 Koppelman.

cleaning a gun — to the extent that you would prefer not to fire the blooming thing.

I had been issued a .30-caliber carbine and was taught that the first thing you did was to make sure you were cleaning your own weapon. Now and then, someone would clean the wrong weapon, and this would really break up everyone else. The fellow whose weapon had been cleaned always thanked the good samaritan profusely.

At one point, I came up with what I considered a brilliant idea. I filed down part of the firing mechanism in the carbine, figuring that I could fire individual shots or just hold down the trigger and fire a burst. When I completed filing down the part, I got some ammunition and tried it out. But there was one problem with my brilliant idea: There was nothing to shut off the firing after it began. Once I squeezed the trigger, I was unable to stop the whole clip from being fired. Sheepishly, I went back to the quartermaster and told him I had a problem with my gun. He had it fixed and I never heard any more about that — for which I guess I was pretty lucky.

Ammunition was extremely scarce, and we were given very little for practice. We went to the rifle range to fire for record, and we were using the bolt-action Springfield rifle. It was rapid fire in different positions,

A visit to Camp Crowder, Missouri, with my brother, Henry.

and as I swung into the prone position, the rifle jammed. The instructor told me to make each shot count and not to worry about getting them all off. Having learned how to fire this rifle, I knew that the sling would bring the gun back on target after each shot. As soon as the sights would drop back onto the bull's-eye, I would fire. The instructor was furious. I didn't say anything, but then the score was raised 200 yards away from the pits. I had hit nine bull's-eyes and one just off the bull. The fellow who pasted targets told me that he could have put his fist over all ten of those holes. The instructor never said another word, and I did get my expert rifleman's bar at that time.

One day they lined up the whole company on the company street. We were all wearing our helmet liners when the quartermaster came along and dropped our steel helmets on top of the helmet liners. The helmet weighed two and three-fourths pounds, and I felt like my head was being pushed down through my shoulders. We were ordered always to wear our helmets from then on. I can well understand why my neck grew more than an inch thicker during the three years I was in the service. It was not long, though, before the helmet became just another piece of wearing apparel and its weight was not a factor.

There was a fellow in another company who was about five feet tall and weighed 240 pounds. He swore that he was not five feet tall but that the draft board had cheated in measuring him. Thousands of dollars were bet on whether or not this fellow would be able to get down the turret of a tank. It certainly surprised me — and a lot of others — when he was able to enter the tank. They assigned a sergeant to him to keep him running, and the last time I saw him, he weighed about 200 pounds and was in great shape.

We were allowed to apply for weekend passes, and sometimes three-day ones. My oldest brother, Henry, was stationed at Camp Crowder, Missouri, which was not very far from Fort Riley. So I applied for a pass and went to visit him. He was an officer in the Signal Corps. I also visited him later on during training. My other brother, Dick, was never near enough to visit until we both were in Europe.

We usually were allowed to go into town on weekends, but one particular weekend, all leaves and passes were canceled and we were confined to the barracks area. Naturally there was plenty of bitching and complaining. Some of the fellows immediately made arrangements with local taxi drivers to deliver booze out to the company area. Kansas was a dry state, but apparently no one had ever told the taxi drivers about it.

Then we were advised that President Franklin D. Roosevelt was to review the troops in dress uniform, but before that, there would be a full inspection of all equipment. By the time they were finished, we were all spit and polish. Finally we were ordered to fall in. We were told that we would march out to the highway near camp and spread out, single file, at arm's length, with fingers barely touching, on one side of the highway. When the presidential cavalcade was due to approach, we would be called to attention, but instead of standing in the attention position, we would place our palms flat against our lower abdomen and remain perfectly still until the president passed by.

Meanwhile, some of the fellows who had been well stocked by the cab drivers began to feel their oats in the hot Kansas sun. When you have to go, you have to go, and even the President of the United States would have had a problem with nature under those circumstances. Civilians being trained to be soldiers do many things to drive officers right up the wall — and we were no different. The CO had a strong heart because he didn't pass out on the spot. Needless to say, we had once again sorely tried his patience.

Leading the presidential limousine was a Jeep, on the hood of which sat a Secret Service agent with a tommy gun. All he did was watch our hands as the entourage drove by. I would have hated to have sneezed at that moment. On the ridge above the road were armed guards that we could see from our vantage point. Ten thousand of us strung out along the highway at arm's length must have covered quite a few miles.

The army also had a nasty little trick that they would pull on us early

Tornado strikes Camp Funston, May 15, 1943.

in the morning. This would occur periodically without any warning. At about five o'clock, we would suddenly be roused from bed and ordered to stand at attention. Parts of most of the men were already at attention, and this was known as a short-arm inspection for venereal disease. The doctor would walk around inspecting each of us — which was never appreciated by anyone.

Although military training was the main objective at Fort Riley, we also experienced the wonders of Kansas weather. One day, one of my buddies called me out on the balcony of the barracks to look at a strange cloud formation. As I walked out, I was intrigued by the massive black cloud, close to the ground, that was approaching. A fellow from Oklahoma asked what we were looking at, and when we pointed to it, he went right over the rail, down the fire stairs, and dove under a culvert in the roadway. He then turned and shouted to us, "You damned fools, get down here. It's a tornado." After we hustled down to join him, that tornado ripped by, totally destroying the row of barracks a block away from ours. I did manage to take pictures of the twister when the funnel was clearly visible. Luckily it hit during a weekend, when most of the men were away on pass. Another one hit the camp later on, but I didn't see it.

One day we had been out training and returned to the barracks as a group. We raced upstairs and found a horrifying scene. Here was one of our buddies hanging by his bound wrists from one of the posts of the barracks, and another fellow was standing there holding a cat-o'-nine-tails, screaming at him. The fellow tied to the post was bare to the waist, and there were huge welts all across his back. We jumped the fellow with the whip and tore it out of his hands. Then the two of them began to laugh. It seems the fellow hanging on the post had such sensitive skin that it was possible to raise huge welts just by running a fingernail across his back. The two of them decided to try it out on us, and they were extremely successful in making us believe it was a real scene of torture.

Another fellow in our company had been a sword swallower with a carnival. He didn't have an Adam's apple, so he could take a whole glass of water and actually dump it down his throat. We could hear the water splash when it hit his stomach. Needless to say, it didn't take much to amuse us.

When we started training, the track vehicles were allowed out on the state highways, but soon afterward, they were forbidden because they were extremely destructive to the pavement. Before that happened, though, a car racing down the highway came up behind one of our tanks and could not brake in time. He struck the tank. About two miles farther down the highway, a state trooper stopped the tank and advised the driver that he had been in an accident. The crew of that thirty-ton tank had not even felt it.

After we were issued half-tracks, every now and then we would throw a track, and it would be a miserable job to put it back on. Our whole crew would get together and jimmy and pry until we finally would get it in place. Not long after that, some genius came up with the idea of inserting a powerful spring that would keep the track under tension and, as a result, keep it from spinning off. This worked beautifully, and I think it is still used on track vehicles.

We endeared ourselves to our company commander by going out on exercises — and, unbeknownst to him, taking along hot dogs and rolls and enjoying a picnic in the process. During one of these picnics, a fellow in uniform walked up to our vehicle and asked what we were doing. We invited him to have a hot dog, but he declined. Then we explained who we were and what we were doing on the exercise. He seemed very interested. When we returned to the company area, we discovered that our company commander had just returned from a meeting with Major General John W. Leonard, commanding officer of our division, who had been impressed with how hospitable we had been but wanted our company commander to explain how that related to our training. As I remember it, the CO had very little sense of humor about this. Our company commander was a real nice guy and technically knew communications, but it wasn't long before there was a change in the company command.

Our training also included hand-to-hand combat — most of which we practiced with wooden guns. I was of the old school, which thought a

McAvoy with helmet liner, gas mask, long johns, and wooden gun. We would joke about these.

good right cross was as good as any fancy judo or jujitsu. I soon learned that I had to pay attention to what they were showing us. One sergeant was an expert tumbler, and he could disarm a man from twelve feet away by going into a tuck and rolling right up to the person he wanted to disarm. We may have had wooden guns, but there was no way of getting that fellow before he was upon you. Our training was more in judo, which was developed by a police commandant in Hong Kong and was very effective in disarming a man carrying a gun or a knife.

We also were given extensive training with the gas mask — definitely not the most pleasant work. The rubber mask was hot, which made me perspire heavily; I never found it very comfortable. We were taken out to a training area where a small amount of mustard gas was released while we were wearing our masks. We were then ordered to remove the masks, and even though the amount of gas was minimal, it still doubled us up with its effects.

We were constantly practicing on our radio sets, copying Morse code being transmitted from other areas, etc. One day I was sitting in the half-track copying code coming in and I couldn't believe what I was writing. In essence, it said, "The lieutenant is a blinkety-blank SOB, etc.," and this went on and on. We speculated that the sender would find himself in trouble up to his eyeballs. When we returned to the company, we asked him what had happened. It seems that the lieutenant was giving him hell

Obstacle course. One slip means one drip.

We earned our $50-per-month pay.

and he thought he had his set off, but he had the exciter plate on, and he was sending in Morse code what he thought of the officer. Luckily enough, the exciter plate generated only enough power to transmit a very short distance, and apparently we were the only ones to pick it up. Needless to say, that log was scrapped immediately.

One night I was returning from the post exchange when I heard a heated discussion between an officer and one of my noncommissioned officers. Both of them were dead drunk. The officer was furious because the sergeant would not salute him. The sergeant was saying that he wouldn't salute any officer he didn't respect. I figured that both of them were so blitzed that they wouldn't remember anything in the morning, so I gave the officer a big salute and then told him that I would take the sergeant with me and report this incident. (The sergeant outranked me.) Since I had given the drunken officer such a beautiful salute — which he returned in a sloppy, drunken manner — he went along with my suggestion. We never heard any more about that, and I didn't even know who the officer was or where he was stationed.

Finally, we were beginning to understand our company's objective in the training of the division. It was our mission to supply all communications between the combat commands and division headquarters. This included radio communications, telephone wire

A latrine rumor starts. Left to right: Waterman, Bradley, McAvoy, Morone, and Lester.

Our troop train somewhere in Colorado.

service, and messenger service. We also had a radio repair platoon. We would form net control stations to integrate all the radio communications from the units to G-2 (intelligence) and G-3 (planning).

Eventually we became very proficient in one of the army's greatest accomplishments — latrine rumors. It was always considered amusing for a group to get together and start a rumor and see how far and to what extent the story would be carried through the troops. This was done so much that you didn't dare believe anything until you had checked it out. Our company boasted some of the finest latrine-rumor initiators ever trained in the service.

In June 1943, we were ordered to move from Fort Riley to Camp Ibis, in the Mojave Desert near Needles, California. We were not ecstatic about moving to the desert for the summer, but war was being fought in the desert of North Africa, and desert training was to be our lot.

From Camp Funston, we were marched to the railroad tracks, where we were loaded onto troop trains that would transport us, without vehicles, to the desert. This involved moving more than 10,000 men by railroad. Our kitchen crews were assigned to baggage cars, where they set up portable kitchens and prepared our meals during the trip. This was the first of three moves by railroad that our division would make during training in the United States.

Las Vegas, Nevada, 1943, from the troop train.

Our first view of beautiful California.

Two

Camp Ibis, California

The troop train arrived at Needles, California, and from there went to the closest railroad point, where we were loaded onto trucks and transported twenty miles into the desert. There, a tented area would be our home for the next five months. Each tent held enough cots to accommodate six men; the tent floors were sand. Throughout the area, latrines and showers were installed in various buildings. These were our luxury accommodations.

We soon found that summer in the desert made for a very different lifestyle. As soon as the sun rose each morning, we would begin to perspire. When we were soaking wet, we would reach a cooling period as the sweat dried. Then, when we were almost dry, we would start to feel tremendously warm and uncomfortable and break into another round of perspiration. This went in cycles all day long, and at the end of the day, we could scrape the salt from the backs of our uniforms. When we began to feel weak, we would take salt tablets, but this did not happen often, because the food was heavily salted. The best drink of the day came from a water bag that had hung all night in the reasonably cool night air. Every morning, I would get up and immediately take a long drink of cool water.

I ended up being assigned to a half-track, which would be the type of vehicle I would have for the rest of my time in the service: It was equipped with a CW (constant wave) Morse code radio and I was trained as a radio operator. At first I qualified as a high-speed radio operator because I could receive and send twenty words per minute. Then the level for a high-speed radio operator was raised to twenty-five words per minute. I could send twenty-five words with a hand key, but I could only write about twenty-three words a minute, so I no longer qualified for the high-speed label. (With a typewriter I could easily do this, but we did not have typewriters.)

At times we would be told to move twenty, thirty, or forty miles from camp and continue to maintain radio communications. One day we headed for Searchlight, Nevada, which was just a few shacks and a gambling place. It was probably the most desolate part of the desert. When we stopped there, we lost contact with our other stations. When

The half-track — our home-away-from-home for most of the rest of the war. Sgts. Millard and Kleingarner. Duane Lester operating the radio; notice sending key attached to right leg.

we moved away from Searchlight, we immediately picked up our other stations again. The gold and other minerals in the ground at Searchlight would draw the radio signals directly into the ground. We soon learned that certain areas are not good for radio transmissions or reception. Searchlight was an amazing town. During the day, the place was dead, but at night the town would really come to life with the gamblers coming across the line from California. It was the hot spot of the desert.

The desert sands had a crust on them, and the first vehicle would have traction and be able to maintain a good speed, but the vehicle following in the same tracks could only move in a slow, grinding pace through soft sand. When we went on maneuvers, this was extremely exhausting to the drivers — the heat of the day, the heat of the engine, and the direct rays of the sun would really drain them. If we attempted to use any tools, they were so hot we had to wear gloves to hold them.

When we could take a half-track out alone in the desert, it was great sport to chase rabbits. The vehicle would scare up the rabbit and we would sit up on the armorplate windscreen and shoot at the creature. The half-track would travel as fast as it could, chasing the rabbit whichever way it went. We never did manage to shoot a rabbit, but we covered a lot of desert. This exercise was not sanctioned by our officers.

The welcoming committee of the desert consisted of sidewinders, desert rattlers, scorpions, Gila monsters, tarantulas, coyotes, and rabbits. And there were cute little lizards everywhere. My personal experience with all of these was that the sidewinders never presented a problem because they are the type of small rattlesnake that doesn't strike but uses your forward motion to sink his fangs into you. Our combat boots

The company street. The first anniversary of the 9th Armored Division.

protected us from these creatures. My one experience with the desert rattler came as we were about to leave the desert and had been ordered to spread out and police the area. I was walking along when my buddy hit me across the chest with a staff. As I turned toward him angrily, he pointed. Directly in my path, and coiled, was a five-foot rattler just waiting for my arrival. As soon as he knew that we had seen him, he began to rattle. We had encircled him when an officer called out to see what we were doing. He came running over and despatched the snake with a rock. Our hero had saved us, and he acted as if he really had. This snake had a body about as thick as my arm and eleven rattles on his tail.

We drew vehicles that were already at the camp and immediately began exercises in desert maneuvers. They started out with just daytime trips and then began getting into overnight and mass maneuvers. The desert heat was said to be about 120 degrees Fahrenheit, and it was exhausting to be in these armored vehicles, in the hot sun, and around the heat of the motors all day and then continue all night. We all carried salt tablets and a limited amount of water.

We went out into the desert on many training exercises, and some of them were overnight. Since there was little if any chance of rain, we would throw our bedrolls down beside the vehicle. One morning, when I

My luxury accommodations on the desert.

went to put on my coveralls, there was a tarantula in them. All three of us — the coveralls, the spider, and I — parted company immediately. That spider was huge. One of the fellows once caught a tarantula and rolled him over on his back. He had two fangs in the middle of his stomach. That didn't look like anything I wanted to associate with.

It was on these maneuvers that most of us came to be aware of or to know Colonel Kelly. He was the chief of staff of the division and had a caustic tongue that could whittle anyone down to size. He delighted in catching staff officers doing something wrong, but he never hesitated to blister an enlisted man for making an error. Colonel Kelly trained our division because there was no officer who was willing to face him after a miscue.

Once, we were operating at night under blackout conditions when two columns crossed each other. Apparently this wasn't supposed to happen. Our vehicle was one of the lead vehicles, and a caustic voice came out of the darkness: "Whose G-d- vehicle is that?" We immediately recognized that it was Colonel Kelly and responded, "149th Armored Signal Company, sir." His response was, "Get that G-d- vehicle out of here." You didn't ask Colonel Kelly how or where — you just got out of there.

*The best of Searchlight,
Nevada, in 1943.*

We were constantly practicing during these times, and some of the exercises involved spreading camouflage nets over the vehicles. These nets had a mesh of about two inches square, and sand-colored webbing was woven through the holes. It made great camouflage, but it was absolutely stifling. There was no movement of air, and all it did was retain the heat. Between operating under the camouflage nets and having all-night exercises without sleep, we all found the maneuvers exhausting.

All the time we were in the desert, we were operating our radios and carrying on exercises. Then, all of a sudden, we received direct orders from Washington to maintain radio silence. This was one of the few times that we received an explanation for an order: It seems that our radio transmissions were interfering with the radio sets in combat areas in North Africa. Radio operates on three waves — ground wave, line of sight, and sky wave. Sky wave was the one causing the trouble. It is unreliable because it bounces from a radio ceiling in the sky that varies in height. That's why, at times, you can receive a station from a distant place and then will never receive it again. Apparently the sky wave had reached a level that allowed our signals to bounce down in North Africa.

We had all been ordered to wear our gas masks, and the desert made this just another hot and sweaty feature. One day, a member of our crew

Sgt. Ike Kleingarner and Duane Lester in exhausted sleep on maneuvers.

was walking near the half-track when I heard a gentle voice say, "Son, where is your gas mask?" I turned and recognized Colonel Kelly. The man responded, "In the half-track, sir." The response from the colonel was explosive: "Well, get the G-d- thing on!" I'll guarantee that he wore that gas mask from then on.

We were on maneuvers down near Danby Dry Lake when two P-51 fighter planes were hedgehopping across the desert. The power lines from Hoover Dam crossed the desert near there, and the first pilot apparently saw the lines and pulled up. The second pilot apparently didn't see them until too late. He tried to pull up, only to have his wing cut right through the cable. I couldn't believe that the cable didn't cut the wing off, rather than the reverse. There was a flash of light around the plane and the motor coughed and then caught, and that pilot headed for home. When the cable was cut, one of the towers supporting the cable also fell. We now had a desert with some pretty hot cables resting on the ground. We posted guards at that area until repair crews could arrive, but I have no idea who, besides us, would have been out there. Danby Dry Lake had the finest sand that I have ever seen. It was impossible to hold that sand in your hand without its sifting through your fingers. Think of driving in stuff like that.

Left to right: Lucas and Waterman with relics of the past; gold mine in the background, Searchlight, Nevada.

During that time, we moved at night under blackout conditions, and one of our routes was down through an arroyo that was just wide enough for our vehicles. What impressed all of us was that all the noise of the tanks and half-tracks failed to drown out the rattles of the rattlesnakes lying in the crevices of those arroyos. We knew that if one of our vehicles broke down, we would be up to our ears in snakes.

Every night the coyotes would howl, but we never did lay eyes on them. For sleeping in the desert, we had comforters instead of bedrolls, and one night three of us bedded down together. One of the fellows was smoking when we all fell asleep. His cigarette fell onto the comforter, and the next thing I knew, I was trying to wake up and gagging with smoke at the same time. I pushed myself up on my elbow and stared at the ring of fire at the top of the bedroll, but I couldn't seem to make a move. Just then, the guard on duty spotted the fire and rousted us. The smoke had doped me to such an extent that I was incapable of acting.

As we were assembling for mess one evening, one of the men called out and we went to see what he had found. When I arrived, about fifteen or twenty fellows had surrounded what I now know to be a Gila monster. It was the ugliest, baggiest animal I have ever seen. The size of it and the rolls of fat were revolting. We had it surrounded, and the men started to

*Outhouses and a gold mine
from the top of the radio
vehicle, Searchlight, Nevada.*

close in. That thing took off so fast that nobody had a chance to move. Luckily enough, it didn't attack anyone: Since then, I have read about how poisonous its bite would have been.

One day while on maneuvers, the whole horizon took on a beige color. It was a strange sight, and we watched with interest. We soon found out that it was a sandstorm — probably the most miserable thing that can happen in the desert. Wind-driven sand stings and hurts. We ducked down behind our vehicle but still couldn't get away from it. I took my tent shelter half and wrapped myself in it, and that helped. Just imagine being hot and sweaty and then getting hit with one of those miserable storms. The sand was down our necks, in our ears, in our shoes, and everywhere else, and we had no water for bathing. Water rationing was strictly enforced: For example, we would get up in the morning and wash, then shave in the water in which we had washed, and then rinse out our socks in the shave water. It didn't leave any water to waste on a bath.

This particular storm lasted between fifteen minutes and a half hour, and it left us with a massive amount of work. The first order of business was to clean all of the equipment, which meant the machine gun as well as the motor of our vehicle. Then we had to check the radio set to be sure

Left to right: Lester and Stine. We played ball in the desert, too.

all the sand was out of it. And, finally, we had to do a general housekeeping of the vehicle itself. Each one of us had to clean our weapons. At the same time, we were on maneuvers, so we also had certain orders we had to follow. I was only in that one sandstorm, but it left a lasting impression.

On the reverse end of things, every now and then we would have violent thunder, but usually no rain accompanied it. One particularly hot day, we noticed storm clouds coming, and then, suddenly, it was pouring rain. We stood there, letting ourselves get soaked. The rain didn't last long, but it was a welcome relief from the heat. The desert, however, takes back everything it gives. The sun came out immediately and the desert was stifling once again. For a short time, the humidity was unbelievable, but then we were back to the old routine of dry heat.

We had orders that no vehicle would be allowed through a bivouac area at night without a man walking in front of the vehicle. This was because we had a lot of heavy equipment, and some of our fellows had been run over. One night I saw a Jeep coming through the area with blackout lights and nobody in front of it. I stepped away from my vehicle and yelled at the driver to get somebody in front of his damned vehicle. I heard a voice say, "All right, sergeant. You walk in front, I'll drive."

When the Jeep came by, I saw that it had two stars on it, and General Leonard was driving. It isn't often that you can give orders to a general — and get away with it.

One night, back at Camp Ibis, I was on guard in the ammunition tent and heard a clicking noise behind me. I flashed my light, but there was no sign of anyone or anything. Naturally, I was curious. Then, suddenly, I flashed my light just in time to see something slide under one of the ammo boxes. I waited, and when it came out, it was a huge scorpion with a body about five or six inches long and a tail to match. My rifle butt took care of that fellow in a hurry.

Other times, when on guard, we were reasonably near the highway, and automobile headlights would appear. It always seemed like an awfully long time before the car would finally race by. There wasn't much else to do, so when car headlights would appear in the distance, I would mentally record the time that I first sighted the headlights (not the glow) and then check the time when the car would go by. The estimated speed of the car would be between sixty and eighty miles per hour, and we could actually see those headlights for as long as forty-five minutes. Being from New England, I found this extremely unusual, as we can only see a car coming for a few miles at most. Guard duty was a boring job, so we tried any kind of activity that would use up the time.

In order to test our communications, we would be ordered to drive in different directions so there would be considerable mileage between our radio vehicles. One day, when we were racing through the desert as fast as we could go, the half-track went off a four-foot drop. It dove into the sand and came to an abrupt halt. Fortunately, the three men in the front of the vehicle were all wearing their helmets, because they hit headfirst into the steel machine-gun bar across the top of the vehicle. I was on the radio. Since I'm right-handed, the wire for the sending key crossed my lap, and the key was attached to my right leg. The wire flipped me like a top, slamming me on my back on the steel floor. I remember lying there and thinking that I should get up, but I wasn't able to move — even though the sun was bothering my eyes. Finally I got up — only to find that the three fellows in the front were out cold. I revived them with a little spray from the water bag, and we continued on our way at a much slower pace.

We drove our half-track out to the moving-vehicle machine-gun range for firing practice. After a time, the lieutenant ordered me to take a couple of men to the target and paste it. (By this time, I was a corporal.) This meant taking little scraps of paper and gluing them over the holes. As we started to glue the targets, we heard a machine gun open fire. I

Left to right: Sgts. Rothermel and
Coombs with machine gun and
ammunition belts.

The Hollywood Canteen on
Cahuenga Street, Hollywood,
California.

Motor pool with barrage balloons in
the distance. "MC" on vehicle stands
for Message Center.

Barrage balloons in case of Japanese
attack.

Left to right: McAvoy, Lucas, Gagerges, and Morone. Five minutes after this picture was taken, the colonel caught us and broke the bottles. The heat of the desert was not the place for a hangover.

didn't pay too much attention, because we were firing at two hundred yards and there was more than one firing range. But then I began to see holes appearing just over my head in the target that I was pasting. I yelled and hit the ground with the other two, and we burrowed like a shot across that desert floor to the Jeep. After the firing stopped, we headed back to the half-track. I was steaming. When we arrived, I jumped out and demanded to know what stupid jerk had been firing that gun. A sergeant grabbed me and tried to walk me away from the vehicle, but I would have none of it. Finally, he yanked me aside and said, "Mac, it was the lieutenant who was firing." I told him that I didn't give a damn if it was the general himself. He then said, "Look, he has made a damned fool of himself in front of the men, and he could be court-martialed. If we drop it, I don't think we will have this guy for long." He was right, because the lieutenant was gone not long after that.

Picnic and outing to Lake Mead broke the monotony. The pass on the right is where Hoover Dam creates this 110-mile lake in the desert.

Just about every noon — when we were either in the mess line or had just gotten our food — a wind devil would strike. These mini-tornadoes would swirl tall columns of sand. Once I even saw an empty cement bag swirling two or three hundred feet in the air. Needless to say, getting a plate full of sand with your food was not appetizing. One noon, a wind devil came right down among the tents, ballooned out the tent next to mine, and split it right in half.

A couple of times we were able to get passes into San Bernardino or Los Angeles and Hollywood. I couldn't believe how cold Los Angeles felt during the summer, and I stopped to look at a thermometer. It was 72 degrees, and I was freezing. We enjoyed the shows at the USO, and I met Frances Langford and Martha Raye at the Hollywood USO. It was about a three-hundred-mile drive in the rear of a truck back to camp, so we stopped at a roadside stand and purchased splits of champagne which were in a cooler. I never did understand what splits of champagne were doing in that rundown old place, but we bought all they had and managed to down them on the way back to camp. I can report now that a hangover and the desert heat do not mix.

From time to time, we also had outings to Lake Mead and Hoover Dam. Lake Mead was a 110-mile body of water created when Boulder (Hoover) Dam was built. We were able to drive across the dam, but for security reasons, no one was permitted to stop. Antiaircraft guns were mounted in strategic positions all around the dam to prevent any enemy aircraft from destroying it.

Our vehicles were kept in what we would now call a motor pool, near the tented area. One day, a thunder-and-lightning storm descended, and

The rugged country about 1/4 mile from Hoover Dam.

lightning struck the motor pool, where some of our men were standing. Some of them were killed and the rest were seriously injured. Two men who were in one of the vehicles were untouched.

While on the West Coast, we were assigned to the Pacific Coast Defense Command. Near our camp was a restricted area covered with barrage balloons. We never did know what was over there, but we could see the balloons. We were awarded the American Theater Campaign Medal for our participation in this defense.

The latrine rumors soon were rampant that we would be on the move to Camp Polk, Louisiana. It seems that the war in North Africa was going very well, and now they wanted to train us in the swamps instead of the desert. Sometimes these latrine rumors turned out to be true, and this was one instance of it. We were ordered to police the area and pack up our gear to board troop trains. We were told to put all of our vehicles in A-one shape to get them ready for the next group scheduled to come in.

Two little Mexican boys greet us in New Mexico.

Three

Camp Polk, Louisiana

I n October 1943, we shipped out of Camp Ibis aboard sleeper cars on a troop train. One man was in the upper berth and two men were in the lower. We found it hard to believe the size of the Southwest desert! It extends from just east of Los Angeles, across Arizona and New Mexico, and halfway across Texas. We traveled across that entire area, heading directly east, and I remember that the train stopped in Dallas, where we were put through a series of exercises and a short march while the train was taking on water. I don't remember how long the trip was, but it took more than a few days. When we arrived at Camp Polk, Louisiana, the weather was absolutely beautiful.

At Camp Polk, we found the barracks already occupied by what the locals called "water bugs." Having been in the hotel business, I knew a cockroach when I saw one, but these were the granddaddies of them all. They were about two inches long and even flapped their wings when they fell from the wall. They loved to hang around the drinking fountain, and taking a drink of water with my eyes about six inches from one of those creatures made a lasting impression on me.

We immediately drew equipment there at the post and then started maneuvers in the area around the camp. The weather stayed beautiful for about a month, but then it began to rain. If I remember correctly, it rained for about six weeks. Our vehicles were out in areas that were becoming boggy, so we cut saplings and laid them in front of the wheels of the half-track so we could drive out of the woods. Being from New England, we figured we had come up with a brilliant solution: We would take the winch at the front of the vehicle, place it around a large pine tree, and winch ourselves out of that swamp. But when we started to pull up on the winch, suddenly that huge pine was falling right toward us. Luckily enough, we were all able to duck in time — before the tree crashed right down over the top of the vehicle. In Louisiana, the trees are rooted in soft soil — not the firm New England soil so familiar to us. We didn't try that trick again. Getting that vehicle out of the swamp meant a massive amount of work.

Around this time, I was granted a furlough to go home to Maine. Trains were pretty much the only transportation available to us, and they

On furlough in Lewiston, Maine, with my mother and Rusty.

were always overcrowded to an extreme. I thought I was lucky when I drew one of the new air-conditioned passenger cars, but it turned out that the air conditioning had broken down. The car had room for about eighty passengers, but another forty were also squeezed in there. It was unbelievably hot and stuffy, and the conductor was a real grouch who refused to do anything about it. After many complaints and no action, there was a terrific crash, and a picture window a few seats ahead of me was taken right out. The conductor came racing into the car with the military police, but of course nobody had seen anything. (At that time, there were MPs assigned to every train.) The air coming in that window was so welcome and such a relief that we all silently thanked whoever had done the deed. The MPs attempted to find out who had done it, but to no avail.

Throughout the trip to Maine, our tickets were checked constantly by the conductor — with an MP to back him up. One time, I was fast asleep in my seat when the conductor woke me up to ask for my ticket. I had stuck it in the clip on the back of the seat in front of me, so I pointed to it. But the conductor demanded that I hand him the ticket. The railroads had brought out of retirement a lot of old, dyspeptic conductors who certainly did nothing for public relations. There was no arguing with them, as the MPs were there to prevent any difficulty, and they would support the conductor.

Upon returning from furlough, I found that the unit was out in the field on maneuvers, so I was given a ride out there. As usual, it was raining — it had been raining since I left. As I walked across the bivouac area carrying my duffel bag, bedroll, helmet, and carbine, it was obvious that the water had risen considerably. There was a stream running through the area, and I started to wade across it. Suddenly I found myself chest-high in water. A slit trench that had been dug there had filled up with water, and I had walked right into it. A fellow relieved me of all my baggage and stepped back, waiting while I tried to extricate myself from the stream. I had hit so solidly into the mud in the trench that I could not move my feet. So a couple of fellows gave me a hand and dragged me out of the water. It was a great homecoming — all of my clothes, my bedroll, and my carbine were soaking wet. Naturally, there was no sun to dry anything. My buddies enjoyed my discomfort tremendously.

While at Camp Polk, we experienced the worst of Louisiana winters, even including an ice storm. One night I was in my pup tent but my buddy hadn't turned in yet. I heard a crack, a snap, and then a swishing noise. A huge branch had become coated with ice and had broken off one of the tall pines. That branch wiped out the other side of my pup tent and buried itself about a foot deep in the ground. I was stunned when the tent pole snapped and hit me on the head. It was a close call. Being from the Northeast, I found it ironic that I should almost be killed in an ice storm in Louisiana.

When we were allowed to build fires, there was plenty of firewood around to make a good one. One day when we were splitting wood, we came upon a coral snake hibernating in a log. The fire took care of that fellow in short order.

Wild pigs — about the size of small dogs — were everywhere, always wandering around our bivouacs attempting to find food, and sometimes rattling the mess kits hanging on the edges of the pup tents. When we expected to be in an area any length of time, we would dig an eight-foot-by-eight-foot hole into which all of the garbage and slop would be dumped. One day, one of the wild pigs fell into the slop pit. Even though the animal was in seventh heaven, he actually was in danger of drowning. So one of the farm boys in our unit went down into the pit and lifted him out. I thought that the guy should have been given either a medal or a Section 8 discharge.

About this time, our vehicle crew was placed on special duty with a unit of black soldiers on maneuvers in the area. We spent two or three weeks with them, supplying them with communications. I don't remember what their assignment was, but we set up permanently and did not move our vehicle after arriving there. This was a real soft deal, a nice change, because we had been used to coping with the continual movement of an armored division. It gave us the opportunity to string an aerial from the trees for better reception and sending power. The regular antennas on the vehicle had a calibrated setting, and we could operate them from the dials on the radio set. By stringing our own antennas, we had to set everything in Rube Goldberg fashion. We would hold down the sending (transmitting) key and then take a lead pencil and hold it close to the antennas. When a spark would jump from the antennas to the lead of the pencil, we would change our setting until we had the strongest spark leaping across the gap. For the remainder of the time we were there, we operated with that setting on the radio.

Training men in the handling and use of heavy equipment has its price, and we lost ninety-nine men here in the States. The losses occurred for a variety of reasons. Some men were shot on the range; there were motor-vehicle accidents; and two tankers even had their tank settle down on them one night while they were asleep in the swamps of Louisiana. Also, a twenty-ton engineering truck slipped off the road and into the swamps, drowning some men.

At about this time, for some strange reason, I was awarded the Good Conduct Medal. I never did find out how this came about or why it was awarded to me, and many others, at that time.

My second Christmas in the service was at Camp Polk, but this time it was among friends who had lived and trained together for the previous thirteen months. We all still had that feeling of wanting to be home for Christmas, but we recognized that there were many men all over the world in the same predicament. We enjoyed Christmas in a quiet way: Each fellow could be alone with his private thoughts.

We were reminded constantly that our equipment had to be in first-class condition at all times, yet, as radio operators, we were forbidden to repair the radio except for minor adjustments (referred to as first-echelon maintenance). One time, I experienced a strange sound from my set and took it into radio repair to have it checked. They returned it to me as being all right. Again I experienced the same thing and again took the set in with the same report. The third time, as I was transmitting, smoke poured out of the top of the set and the set blew. I took it back to radio repair and told them what happened. Soon my master sergeant came to get me to take me to the CO. He remarked that I was in deep trouble, telling me that the master sergeant in charge of radio repair had taken my set to the CO and was demanding that the man responsible for the loss of that $900 set should pay for it. When I told my sergeant how many times I had taken the set into radio repair, he almost jumped with glee. We

CARRICO WARNS OF DUDS;

MILITARY TRAINING CHIEF URGES CARE IN EXPLOSION AREA

Says Mark All Shells And Telephone 1738

Carrico Warns—
(Continued from Page 1)

at Rifle Range 2. Anyone discovering unexploded shells in any of the on limits areas should flag them and report them immediately to Lt. Edward C. Rudis, ammunition officer, at telephone 1738.

"In no event should unexploded shells be touched. They will be disposed of by competent personnel detailed to clean up the area."

A warning to keep out of the off limits area in the vicinity of the Polk magazine area, scene of fire and explosion last Friday evening, and to leave unmolested any unexploded shells found outside the off limits area was issued this week by Lt. Col. Homer E. Carrico, Chief of the Post military training division.

"With hundreds of unexploded shells lying about the vicinity of the ammunition area," said Col. Carrico, "all personnel are warned to be extremely careful.

"Off limits to all personn .r-ing the emergency is the area ..om the unimproved road just North of Rifle Range 2 to, but not including, the 1000-inch Machine Gun Range on the Small Arms Range.

"Duds are laying on Artillery Road passing the infiltration course, and others are known to have been hurled beyond the hill

(Continued on Page 4, Column 5)

arrived at the CO's office and the radio-repair sergeant made his demand that the man responsible pay for the set. My sergeant agreed that the one responsible should pay and then asked the radio-repair sergeant to produce the log showing how many times the set had been in for repairs. It seems that a field mouse had built a nest in the back of my set, and the nest material was causing some changes in the sound. Obviously, radio repair had not opened the set either time that I had taken it in to them. The third time, the mouse had been walking across the electrodes just as I was transmitting, and I had electrocuted him and blown the set at the same time. Luckily, the records showed that radio repair had received my set and mentioned the problem I had noted. I felt as if I had dodged a bullet on that one, too.

Some time in January, the weather cleared. With nice, sunny days, we began to enjoy baseball and softball during recreation hours. It can be very pleasant in Louisiana when the ground dries out and it's possible to get back to a normal life.

One evening, while we were standing in the mess line, there was a tremendous explosion. All of us were staggered by the concussion. A

EXPLOSION IS PROBED

CLEARANCE OF AREA BEING DIRECTED BY BALLISTICS EXPERT

No Casualties In Fire Of Spontaneous Origin

Clearance Of Area—

(Continued from Page 1)
telligence officer and board recorder.

Other members of the investigating group include Lt. Col. Franklin T. Mikell, Camp executive officer, president; Lt. Col. Homer E. Carrico, Chief of the military training division; Lt. Col. Edwin S. Burt, Post provost marshal; and Capt. Roy J. Qualls, officer in charge of the Post armament, automotive and instrument shops.

Felt In DeRidder

No one was injured in the mishap which shook buildings as far away as Lee Hills and felt as far as DeRidder with the first blast at 5:55 p. m. This first violent explosion was believed caused by 4.2 inch mortar shells detonated by the fire. The second and third big blasts came at 6:27 and 6:58 p. m., respectively, and their origin had not been established definitely by the investigators on Tuesday.

The second explosion left both camps without lights, and sent a huge smoke ring towering to a height estimated by pilots at the Polk landing strip at more than 2,000 feet, holding together for more than 10 minutes.

The power was cut when a fragment from a 105 mm. shell severed one strand of the power line. Service in North Camp was restored Friday night after the main switch between camps was pulled, but not in time for opening of theaters, PXs and the Service Club. Power was restored in South Camp Saturday morning when the break was repaired by linemen from the Louisiana Power and Light Company.

Heat Believed Cause

Originating in ammunition supplies stored under canvas outside the storage igloos and believed caused by spontaneous combustion under the 94-degree heat of the Louisiana sun, the fire had been discovered by three 1880th Service Unit MPs before the initial explosion, according to Mr. Zeiders.

The MPs, Pvt. Sam Bailey who was the mounted patrol on duty, and Pvts. Robert H. Murphy and Clifton J. Morales, gate guards, were all standing at the main gate, Mr. Zeiders said, when they saw smoke which they first believed was rising from the infiltration course.

Following a few isolated and muffled explosions, however, they went to the top of the first igloo to investigate and saw that the smoke rose from the back side of the magazine area. The flames were first noticed by Murphy who called the fire department from the guard house outside the gate.

The alarm was turned in at Fire Station 1 at 5:50 p. m. and five minutes later one fire truck had already responded and was approximately 150 yards inside the magazine area on its way to the blaze when the first explosion forced the firemen to withdraw.

Camp officials and MPs went into action immediately, closing the area to the curious and checking to be sure that there were no casualties. Two fire trucks remained ready for action, but at a safe distance, until it became obvious there was nothing the firemen could do.

Explode For Hours

HE shells and small arms ammunition continued to burst for hours following the first blast as the fire was spread to other stores. The last reported HE shell to detonate exploded at 12:20 Saturday afternoon.

Shells were hurled over 1000 yards from the area in some instances, traveling to the East and North. Artillery Road passing the infiltration course was covered with shells and others went beyond the hill on the far side of rifle range 2 where a group of 1880th Headquarters Section men from Camp Headquarters were firing the rifle for record.

This range was peppered with fragments by the first explosion, and many of the men brought souvenirs of their experience back with them when they were able to leave the range. All 40 of the group agreed that they had received an idea of what it is like to be under fire.

Two craters were left by the explosions. The larger, 52 feet wide and 13 to 15 feet deep, marks the site where the 4.2 inch mortar shells, 2,856 of them, had been stored. The smaller crater measures 20 feet across and about six feet deep.

The task of clearing the Polk ammunition area, scene of a fire and three violent explosions last Friday evening, and the surrounding areas got under way Wednesday under the direction of Ferdinand F. Glomb, ballistics expert sent on from Eighth Service Command Headquarters at Dallas.

Meanwhile, a probe of the fire was continued throughout the week by a five-man board appointed Monday by Col. J. K. Boles, Camp commander, to investigate the damage and determine the cause of the mishap which resulted in loss of a large quantity of ammunition but no casualties.

Although the loss has been inventoried, the board was unable to place a dollar value on the damage nor estimate the destruction in tons of explosives, according to WOJG Cloyd E. Zeiders, Post In-
(Continued on Page 4, Column 6)

Two Igloos Wrecked

Spreading rapidly, the explosions wrecked two igloos. Another igloo miraculously escaped damage when a shell pierced the door but failed to explode.

Assisting at the outset of the investigation were Capt. C. B. Ford, Jr., Ordnance Department safety and security officer from Chicago, and Capt. Pitser H. Garrison, special investigator from the security and intelligence division at Dallas.

Closed during the first of the week were the infiltration course, submachine gun range and rifle range 2, but every effort was being made to clear these ranges of duds so that they could be opened before the end of the week.

My oldest brother, Henry, and I met up in the spring of 1944, when he was a lieutenant. I would meet my other brother, Dick, under vastly different circumstances later.

railroad car full of 105mm shells had been sitting on a siding and apparently had become overheated in the summer sun and exploded. The shells continued to explode throughout the evening, and I went to a movie on the post. In the middle of the show, all the doors of the theater blew open and the building swayed back and forth. One of the shells had hit the mortar dump and blown that up. Most of us figured that we didn't need to see the rest of the show. Those shells continued to explode during the night, so the area around the ammunition dump was closed off.

Camp Polk was somewhat different from the other camps we had been in because it had a prisoner-of-war section. We would see the prisoners being taken to work on nonwar projects, and we did remark that they looked well cared for. Little did we know that in the near future, we would see firsthand that American prisoners of war were not accorded similar treatment.

One day I reached into my bag and my hand immediately felt like it was on fire. I had no idea what had hit me but was damned sure I was going to find out. I kicked the bag over and the flap folded back. I saw nothing. Then I flipped the flap over and found a little scorpion waving his tail at me. I took care of him in a hurry and headed for the medic. I was ordered to rest and not exercise for twenty-four hours, until the poison

REPRESENTATIVES OF ALLIED PRESS SEE 9th ARMORED IN PEASON RANGE TANK ATTACK

Correspondents Stop Here On Tour of Camps

Repeating its performance of a month ago for representatives of the press, radio and other publication and pictorial services, the 9th Armored Division this week demonstrated the striking power of an armored division in attack for 19 representatives of the allied press.

The visit of news writers, correspondents, photographers and others, who were accompanied by a number of Army officials from Washington, was part of a tour of military installations.

The visiting party arrived at DeRidder Army Air Base from New York and Washington Sunday night aboard two army transport planes, and proceeded to North Camp.

MacPhail Heads Party

Heading the delegation of Army officials was Lt. Col. L. S. MacPhail, better known to baseball fans as Larry MacPhail, former mentor of the Brooklyn Dodgers, and Major Renato Froncillo, both from the office of the Under Secretary of War; Major John T. Parker, Jr., War Department

(Continued on Page 4, Column 7)

followed its course. Apparently it attacked my nervous system, because my stomach was twitching for a while. I guess I was lucky that the scorpion was little, and not the size of the one I had killed on the desert.

While we were practicing all phases of our operations, we were given the news that we would be putting on demonstrations for the Russians and for the press. This demonstration was to be a mock attack by aircraft doing low-level strafing and bombing of positions just yards in front of our troops, and then we would open up with artillery and tanks and move in to take the position. The Russians were with our observers, who called in the field-artillery shells. When the observer ordered the shelling stopped, the Russian sneered that he certainly hadn't brought it in very close. So the observer immediately called for the artillery to start walking their shells in toward the observation post. The observer went and sat down after telling the Russian to let him know when he had had enough. The observer had decided that he would not stop the shelling, and when the shrapnel started whistling around the observation post, the Russian finally asked that it be

Representatives of the allied press last week saw and fired the weapons of an armored division in a demonstration by the 9th Armored, and later witnessed these weapons in action in a highly realistic tank attack on an enemy position staged by the 9th at Peason Ridge artillery range. The correspondents tried their hand at firing many of the weapons including the carbine (left). During the attack they saw armored medics go into the lines in a half-track (center) to evacuate the crew of a tank disabled by a direct artillery hit and administer plasma (right) while waiting for the ambulance to return. (Official U. S. Army Signal Corps photos)

stopped. The observer mentioned that he would have let those shells go right up his rear end if the Russian hadn't cried uncle.

Another lieutenant suddenly was removed from our company, although he was not over our section. They had discovered that his private motor vehicle showed the red color of the gas that was available only for our military vehicles. Obviously, he had taken a few liberties with government supplies, and I suspect that someone in the motor pool didn't like him.

We were awakened early in the morning on D day — June 6 — and advised that a full-scale invasion of Europe was in progress. Most of us were pretty quiet when this was announced, as all of us, one way or another, had relatives involved. My brother Dick was with the 29th Infantry Division, and this was one of the units that landed during those first days. Almost everyone was glued to the radio to hear the latest news.

We would receive weekend passes that would get us out to Barksdale Field in Shreveport or Baton Rouge or Lake Charles, where we could go swimming. We would get to those places by hitchhiking, since most people were willing to pick up GIs. Hitchhiking was almost a way of life during the war.

FASCINATED AUDIENCE SEES 9th IN COMBAT ACTION AND FINDS IT A DRAMATIC SHOW

The 9th Armored Division, utilizing its enormous firepower to excellent advantage, put on a combat firing demonstration last Saturday afternoon that made a profound impression on general officers and other officers now in the Louisiana maneuver area.

Many officers in the large crowd gathered around Peason artillery tower No. 2, never before had seen an armored division in action. Saturday they saw a well-balanced combat team, including sharpshooting 105 millimeter howitzers, fast-moving medium tanks and infantrymen in half-tracks, and marvelled at the punch the team contained.

The 9th Armored's display was the climax event of an all-day demonstration that included some eye-opening strafing and bombing by a tactical air division.

Like Actual Battle

The demonstration was so realistic that the spectators easily could imagine they were witnessing an actual battle. Fighter planes skimmed low over the targets, the infantry began infiltrating, the big guns opened up and the tanks began their assault. Over the "battlefield" rose great clouds of smoke, punctuated by flashes of exploding shells. Pressure from the explosions could be felt in the crowd.

Before the 9th Armored's team went into action, Col. Thomas L. Harrold, commander of the division's Combat Command A, explained to the officers, many of them from regular infantry units.
(Continued on Page 3, Column 1)

LEONARD THANKS 9th FOR DEMONSTRATION

Pleased By Showing Before Allied Press

Maj. Gen. John W. Leonard, commanding general of the 9th Armored Division, in an address to the personnel of the division, last week expressed his gratification for the splendid discipline, confidence and cooperation displayed by both individuals and units participating in the demonstration given for the representatives of the Allied Press on May 15.

This was the second such demonstration by the 9th, the first being presented a month earlier for 40 representatives of the press and radio in this country while on a tour of army installations.

Harry F. Kern, war and foreign correspondent for the magazine NEWSWEEK, writing about the first tour said:

"They (the ground forces) have recently regained in public esteem their position of preeminence on the battlefield. The two divisions visited, the 9th Armored and the 100th Infantry, showed this. They are keenly officered and at a physchological peak. They are ready for battle in a spiritual sense, as their officers put it."

Correspondents—
(Continued from Page 1)

Bureau of Public Relations; Major Walter L. Stewart, Army Ground Forces; and Capt. Sam S. Woo Army Air Forces.

The newsmen included representatives of Australian, British, Canadian, Chinese, Swedish and other Allied news services.

Monday morning the group was conveyed to the Peason Ridge Artillery Range where they were guests for luncheon and at a series of realistic demonstrations by the 9th Armored, commanded by Maj. Gen. John W. Leonard. Others attending included Maj. Gen. Frank W. Milburn, commanding general of XXI Corps, and members of his staff, Maj. Gen. William M. Grimes, commanding general of the 8th Armored Division, Maj. Gen. Roscoe B. Woodruff, commander of the 84th Infantry Division "Railsplitters" at Camp Claiborne, and Col J. K. Boles, Camp Commander of Camp Polk.

Realistic Demonstration

The morning event was a demonstration of all the weapons that make up an armored division's fire power.

Highlight of the visit was the afternoon demonstration showing how an armored division, in coordination with other branches, sets up and carries out an attack against an enemy objective. Cooperating in this event were 12 P-Warhawks and 24 B-26 bombers the Second Tactical Air Division which strafed and bombed the objective in softening up operations before the attack.

This was followed by artillery fire preparation and then the highly realistic attack in which almost actual battle conditions were demonstrated for the benefit of the visitors. The latter saw how tanks are hit by direct artillery and anti-tank fire, how casualties are rescued from the wrecked vehicles and removed from the field of battle for medical attention, and how attacking tanks fall victim to mines, as well as other realistic eventualities that might develop in actual battle.

Night Firing

The visitors witnessed another spectacular event Monday night when the 9th Armored presented a night firing demonstration. This was a continuation of the afternoon tank attack, in that the attacking forces had dug in for the night and prepared for a counterattack by the enemy.

A demonstration on the night infiltration course concluded the events planned for the visitors who left North Camp Tuesday for the DeRidder Air Base where they resumed their tour.

One time when I was hitching with McWhirter, a young woman stopped and asked if either one of us could drive. McWhirter could, so we responded in the affirmative. She replied, "Fine, I'll get in the back and go to sleep. Wake me up when we get there." That was the best ride we ever had in the service. It was like having our own car.

Another time, we were going to Houston when two men picked us up. The driver wanted to talk. The problem was that he was traveling at about eighty miles an hour, and he kept turning and looking at us in the back seat. We kept leaning over the front seat to talk to him so he could keep his eyes on the road. He was not the best of drivers.

Passes were handed out liberally at Camp Polk, and we really took advantage of them to travel to most of the cities in the area. The rule was

Camp Polk, Louisiana, June 9, 1944

D DAY ANNOUNCEMENT
RECEIVED CALMLY HERE

LITTLE EXCITEMENT
DISPLAYED AS NEWS
BREAKS AT REVEILLE

that you would go about seventy-five miles on a weekend pass and about two hundred miles on a three-day pass. (I don't remember the exact mileage, but that's close enough.) A few fellows from the Cleveland area managed to work out a deal that was supposed to be a beauty. They arranged a three-day pass starting on a Monday, then they got a weekend pass, which would start Friday evening, and then they got some special time off that started on Thursday. They left camp and drove to Cleveland and were gone almost a week. If they had been asked for their papers, they would not have been able to justify being in Cleveland, but the chances of that were pretty slim. Unfortunately for them, the car broke down on the return trip. When that happened, they realized they would be late arriving back at camp, so they telephoned. When they told the CO where they were, the proverbial nitrogenous waste hit the fan. After that, all passes were closely scrutinized and the distance from camp was rigidly enforced. We had to make the CO feel that he was earning his pay.

Rumors were a way of life in the barracks, but one time it was more than a rumor. A notice was posted that an advance cadre would be leaving for England to prepare for the arrival of our division. We now knew where we were heading. Equipment that we were to take with us was to be packed up, but all of the motor vehicles had to be repainted and put in A-one condition for the next unit that would take our place at Camp Polk. When we went down to the motor pool to repaint the vehicles, one of the fellows handed another guy a can of fire-engine-red paint. He did it as a joke, knowing the guy was color-blind. We were sailing along in great shape when I heard someone holler, "What in hell are you doing?" Here was a half-track with one side already painted like a fire truck. We scrambled to get turpentine and get that vehicle cleaned off before an officer spotted it.

With all of our equipment having been shipped, and with little to do, we ended up playing baseball and softball every day. One of our buddies broke his ankle in one of these games, and we left him behind when we shipped out. We finally caught up with him in Germany months later.

The officers usually tried to find something for us to do, and one of the best things to occupy us was training films. They had one film that showed how to avoid contracting a venereal disease, and the film showed a beautiful young girl seducing a soldier. After the film was over, we all agreed that she would have had no difficulty seducing any one of us.

We couldn't find much else to do until one of the fellows who had been roaming around discovered a barracks set up with typewriters and learn-to-type textbooks. So a group of us would go to that barracks every morning and teach ourselves how to type. I was delighted to be able to learn, even though I had a poor teacher. We treated this as a required class, and it worked out very well. The typing I learned there has helped me throughout my business career.

Finally, in August 1944, orders arrived for us to board the troop trains once again, but this time we went to Camp Kilmer, New Jersey. We had been in the Mojave Desert and in Louisiana during the summer, yet the hottest blooming place of all was Camp Kilmer — in New Jersey!

Just before we departed Camp Polk, General Leonard ordered the division to assemble on the parade grounds. We marched into position and public-address systems were in place so we would all be able to hear him. He spoke to us about our becoming a part of the war in Europe and called on all of us to remember three things: our faith in God, our belief in our country, and our sense of humor. Of course we agreed with the first two, but we made quite a case out of the sense-of-humor part of it. It certainly was true, though.

On the trip up to New Jersey, when the train stopped for water in one of the southern states, a black man was passing the train with a wagon full of watermelons. We called out to him, he drove over, and we bought that whole wagonload from him for twenty-five cents a melon. Grinning from ear to ear, he said, "Wait for me and I'll go get another wagonload." Unfortunately, there was no waiting, but at least we all enjoyed some excellent watermelon.

When we reached Richmond, Virginia, we dismounted from the train and marched around the city for a number of blocks just to loosen up. It actually felt good to get off that train and do a few exercises. Then we headed for Camp Kilmer to await orders to board ship for Europe.

Our division had never been known to pass up a chance for a beer or two, so the evening we arrived at Camp Kilmer, we hit the PX — only to have the supply run dry by 10:30 p.m. That almost caused a riot. After dire predictions and threats, the PX the next night had a full supply that didn't run out. I often wondered how much beer was consumed that first night.

It is only fair to mention that handling heavy equipment during extreme summer heat creates a thirst that is hard to quench. Whether or not beer was the best way to quench thirst might be argued, but everyone had a thirst that had to be satisfied. When we were in the desert, there had been no beer available, and no ice either. I suppose some of the men believed in making up for lost time.

We stayed in Camp Kilmer for about a week or so under strict security. Finally we were allowed to spend an evening off the base, and almost everyone headed immediately for New York City. I had relatives in New Jersey, at Lyndhurst, so I told the fellows I would visit my relatives and then meet them in Times Square at midnight. After visiting my relatives and calling home, I headed for New York. When I reached Times Square, at first I didn't see my buddies. Then, when I did, I wished that I hadn't. There were about eight of them, and they were loaded to the gills. They immediately tried to get me to catch up with them, but meanwhile, one of them — a fellow six feet four and a half — was in the midst of an altercation with an MP. The MP wasn't the smartest guy in the world, and he was making matters worse. Finally, I got between the two of them and told the MP to butt out and let me handle these guys. I think he must have been glad to be rid of us, because he certainly didn't have to do what I said. All of a sudden, I found I was the mother hen for these birds, and it was a full-time job herding them into the buses to take us back to camp. I can't say I enjoyed that evening very much.

One of the last training sessions we had was learning how to abandon ship. There were three- or four-story-high structures that would allow us to climb up and then simulate going over the side on rope nets that theoretically would reach down to the water. I never did appreciate heights, and I certainly did not enjoy those exercises. I knew they were necessary, but that didn't mean I had to enjoy them.

Four

The Queen Mary

(Note: This chapter contains excerpts from R.M.S. Queen Mary, 50 Years of Splendour, *by David F. Hutchings.)*

The Board of Directors of the Cunard Steamship Company, Limited, conceived the idea of a huge luxury liner in 1926. Cunard's flagship liner, the *Lusitania*, had been sunk at the outbreak of World War I. After the war, ambitious European and American maritime companies challenged Britain's historic domination of ocean travel.

To meet this challenge, the Cunard Line decided to build the world's largest, fastest, and most glamorous ocean liner. Final blueprints called for a magnificent 81,237-ton vessel, measuring 1,019 1/2 feet from stem to stern and powered by engines capable of maintaining a cruising speed of 28 1/2 knots.

Lacking an official name, the project was simply dubbed "Job #534." John Brown & Company, Ltd., of Clydebank, Scotland, was contracted to build the ship. On December 1, 1930, the first rivet was driven into the longest keel ever laid in a British shipyard.

Then catastrophe struck: The Great Depression devastated Britain's economy, and on December 12, 1931, all work on Job #534 came to an abrupt halt. For more than two years, the unfinished hull stood like a rusting monolith. For twenty-seven long, hard months, the liner lay rusting on the stocks, accumulating 130 tons of rust as well as countless nests of birds that found the manmade cliffs of steel an ideal breeding place.

Smoke and mist hung in a pallid veil over the quiet, hungry town, the usual staccato rhythms of riveting silenced — a silence that spread the meaning of unemployment to all corners of the country.

But in one corner, in the Chamber of the House of Commons, this silence was challenged. David Kirkwood, Labour Member of Parliament for Dunbarton Burghs, demanded the resumption of work on Job #534 to alleviate the unemployment in his constituency. He said, "I believe that as long as Number 534 lies like a skeleton in my constituency, so long will the depression last in this country. To me it seems to shout Failure!

Failure! to the whole of Britain...." At first his cries went unheeded, but gradually sympathetic ears listened to his pleas and took up his cause.

The problem was how to finance the project. The government refused to subsidize Cunard, and Cunard could not afford to restart work with only its own resources. After lengthy and complex discussions, a solution was found, and the government agreed to extend a repayable loan to Cunard — under certain conditions.

The approval of a loan to build an express ship was in itself most unusual in that all foreign competition to 534 had been built with state aid and had been, or would be, run with state subsidies — the ships themselves being loss-makers for the sake of being prestigious. Not only would 534 be paid for from private capital (albeit via a loan), but it would be run on a profitmaking basis, making her unique among her contemporaries.

To add to the financial complexities of the government loan to Cunard, it was stipulated, as part of the agreement, that the company should also take over the ailing White Star Line. This steamship line, founded in 1867, had operated many fast and famous ships in the late nineteenth century, but the company had not always built with an eye to size and comfort. In 1927, the White Star Line became purely British when it was purchased by the Royal Mail Steam Packet Company, adding to its vast empire of interwoven shipping companies. Because of the complexity of its financial structure, RMSP found itself in difficulty, and White Star once again was offered for sale. Cunard was interested but was dubious about the financial pitfalls that would accompany the purchase, and the company backed off. Then the British government stepped in to champion White Star, making merger a condition of the loan to Cunard. Thus, Cunard White Star Ltd. came into existence. Cunard consoled itself with the fact that the company now had £9.5 million — £3 million to complete 534, £1.5 million to provide working capital for the new company, and a further £5 million for the construction of a long-awaited sistership to the liner already under construction.

So, on Tuesday, April 3, 1934, four hundred men, led by two kilt-clad pipers, marched through the jubilant streets of Clydeside back to the open gates of the John Brown shipyard to start clearing the rust from the hull of #534. On May 26, the yard received formal notice to restart construction. Thus, the efforts of David Kirkwood, MP, along with the shrewd business acumen of Sir Percy Bates, had brought about the impossible dream — the mammoth liner was to be completed.

From the time of her conception, #534 was planned as the ship of the age — "The Wonder Ship." Everything about her was to be big, in both quantity and quality. This chapter recounts a few of the statistics and superlatives that made her what she was.

One famous illustration showed the ship with her bows in Whitehall, her starboard bridge wing almost dislodging Nelson from his column in Trafalgar Square, and her stern creating mayhem at the Coliseum Theatre in St. Martin's Lane. In my hometown of Littleton, New Hampshire, if #534 were placed with her stern against the town building, her prow would be beyond the library at School Street, and there isn't a building in town that would be as high as the first open deck from the water (not counting steeples, towers etc.).

Number 534 cost £5 million, and she was the first liner to be more than 1,000 feet long. (The White Star Line had a thousand-footer on the stocks, but the order was canceled, and the French pipped the British at the post when their Normandie was finished — she had been subsidized by the French government throughout the years of depression.) Number 534 would be 1,019 1/2 feet in overall length, with a beam of 118 feet.

During construction, the hull on the stocks embodied 35,500 tons of steel by the time of launching. The stern frame alone weighed 190 tons and the rudder 180 tons, and ten million rivets (4,000 tons) held the vessel together. The plates forming the hull and decks measured from eight to thirty feet in length and weighed from three hundredweight to three tons each. Seventy thousand gallons of paint were needed to cover the outer hull. Two thousand portholes and windows were cut into her sides, requiring 2,500 square feet of thick, strengthened glass.

The liner had twelve decks and was divided into 160 watertight compartments. The distance from the keel to the top of the forward funnel was 184 feet, the funnel was 30 feet in diameter, and the distance between each funnel was 138 feet. The whistles, two on the forward funnel and one on the middle funnel, were six feet seven inches long and weighed one ton each. The beautiful, deep-throated note (more like a roar) that exuded from these whistles could be heard at least ten miles away, and it never failed to thrill.

To propel the ship, four twenty-foot-diameter, four-bladed propellers were fitted, each costing 7,000 British pounds. These were made from fifty-ton "Turbiston" castings, which took fourteen days to cool. The final propellers each tipped the scales at thirty-five tons, which made them the largest propellers made, to that date, by ten tons.

The propellers were driven by four sets of quadruple-expansion, reduction-geared turbines, each having 257,000 blades, all hand set. Developing 50,000 horsepower, they turned at 3000 rpm — this speed being decreased to 200 rpm at the propellers by a reduction gear that was

Spectators on the banks of the Clyde opposite the John Brown shipyard had a magnificent view of the Queen Mary's *launching — even if some of them did get their feet wet.*

itself fourteen feet in diameter. The steam for the engines was provided by twenty-four Yarrow-type water-tube boilers fueled by oil from tanks holding 75,000 gallons, providing water pressure of 400 pounds per square inch. Low-pressure steam for heating and cooking was provided by three double-ended Scotch boilers. Power to light the 30,000 electric light bulbs, operate the twenty-two lifts, 596 clocks, etc., was supplied by seven turbo-generator sets that developed 10,000 kilowatts (enough to power a town of 150,000 people) and was distributed through the ship by 4,000 miles of electrical wire.

The ship could be secured by the then-largest anchors at sixteen tons each, their cables (chains) of 165 fathoms (990 feet) a further 145 tons. The anchor cables, along with other cables and wire hawsers, would measure four miles if laid end to end.

For the safety of passengers and crew, twenty-four lifeboats were carried, twenty of which were thirty-six feet long and twelve feet wide and had a capacity of 145 people.

Passenger capacity was 776 in cabin (first) class, 784 in tourist (second), and 579 in third. To look after the safety and welfare of the ship and her passengers, there were 1,101 officers and crew.

It has been reliably reported that the selection of the name for #534 came about when a small delegation from Cunard Line called on King George V to ask his permission to name their new superliner after Queen

Three funnels fitted and painted in Cunard White Star colors show that the Queen Mary *is nearing completion.*

Victoria. All Cunard ships had had names that ended with -ia, so Victoria would have been a perfect choice. The spokesman opened the conversation with His Majesty by saying something to the effect that Cunard wished to name its new superliner after England's greatest queen. Queen Mary, who was present on this occasion, smiled and said, "I would be delighted."

On September 26, 1934, more than 200,000 people were at the launching, and for the first time it was being broadcast over the radio to an eager nation. The king and queen and HRH the Prince of Wales attended the launching. In his speech, the king said, "Today we come to the happy task of sending on her way the stateliest ship now in being." After his speech, the queen then stepped forward and named the ship, ending years of popular speculation. Because of the well-kept secret, the letters of the liner's name had not yet been riveted to the hull.

"I am happy," the queen said clearly in her first public speech, "to name this ship *Queen Mary*. I wish success to her and to all who sail in her." Then, with a pair of golden scissors, the queen cut a pink ribbon that sent a bottle of Australian wine arcing across the void between platform and ship to shatter against the towering knife edge of the *Queen*

The Mary's *stern is eased into the River Cart as her nose is maneuvered seaward.*

Mary's bow. The queen then turned to the king and asked, "Was that right?"

Then the queen pressed the first of two electric buttons that set in motion the results of four years of complicated calculations and model experiments. Six triggers — which had been holding back the *Mary*'s 35,500-ton launch weight on the inclined slipway — were released. The second button, when pressed, started six hydraulic rams that began to push the gray-painted ship backward on her sliding cradle with an ever-increasing speed toward the River Clyde.

As the liner's bow, still encased in its wood-and-steel cradle, dipped from the edge of the slipway into the river, 2,350 tons of drag chain, connected in bundles to various points along the giant hull, crashed and slid in clouds of rust after the liner, their great bulk and resistance gently bringing the *Queen Mary* to a halt. It had been calculated that the liner would, on this first and perhaps most critical journey of her career, travel 1,194 feet before being brought to a halt. In fact, she traveled just two feet more than calculated, a marvelous verification of the naval architect's art.

Between the 100 seconds of her first faltering movement and the time that she was brought to a halt, she had a tumultuous reception from the spectators — even those who had tried to keep clear of the resulting

The Queen Mary *makes her triumphant entry into New York Harbor, June 1, 1936.*

flood-wave that hit the opposite shore. Then King George and Queen Mary descended from the platform to meet the men who had built the *Queen*. RMS (Royal Mail Ship) *Queen Mary* had been launched.

The liner was towed gently to her fitting-out berth, which would be her home for the next eighteen months while engines, boilers, and many thousands of other items were fitted.

On May 12, 1936, the flag of John Brown (the builder) was lowered in a brief ceremony, and the Cunard White Star Line flags were raised as the *Queen Mary* was officially handed over to her owners.

At teatime (4:30 p.m.) on May 27, the *Queen Mary* left the Ocean Dock in Southampton to begin her maiden voyage. Again, thousands crowded the shoreline and followed the liner in a white flurry of accompanying pleasure craft of all kinds — yachts, motorboats, and paddlesteamers all jockeying for position in an attempt to keep up with the liner as she headed down Southampton Water, past the Isle of Wight, toward Cherbourg (where she was delayed two hours), and then on to New York.

On June 1, 1936, the *Queen Mary's* arrival in New York proved to be one of the most spectacular in that port's history, with a flotilla of craft and airships following the liner in. Cheering crowds and bands waited

The Mary *is welcomed to her American home at Pier 90.*

on the quayside, and the crew was feted for days afterward by jubilant New Yorkers, either in their homes or in public.

The *Queen Mary* vied with the French liner *Normandie* for top transatlantic speed honors, but finally the *Queen* took the record, with a westbound crossing of 30.99 knots and an eastbound one of 31.69 knots — almost a half knot better than the French liner. The *Queen* reigned supreme. But the luxury of speed was also expensive, as the *Mary* burned 1,300 to 1,400 tons of oil per day at speed instead of 1,000 tons per day at normal steaming. Cunard officials also had said sometime earlier that the *Mary* eventually would be run at high speed on the odd occasion in order to glean valuable information for use in the construction of her sistership, #552 (the *Queen Elizabeth*), which also would be built on the Clyde.

By 1939, the sinister specter of nazism had spread its insidious cloak from Germany to cover other states in Europe. Although Neville Chamberlain had stood in front of newsreel cameras and victoriously waved his piece of paper promising "peace in our time," realists knew that a war with Germany was imminent if the Third Reich was to be stopped.

By August of that year, Americans were leaving Europe in droves, returning to the United States in fully booked ships. The *Queen Mary* would sail westward packed to capacity but would return almost empty.

Meanwhile, even as the *Queen Mary* was heading toward Southampton after leaving New York on August 23, Hitler signed his

The Queen Mary *sailed as a luxury liner for just over three years, until she was laid up on September 4, 1939. War had been declared the day before.*

nonaggression pact with Stalin. Passengers aboard the *Queen* expected at any moment to hear that war had been declared. The liner arrived back in Southampton on Monday, August 28, to find that war had not yet been declared, and she sailed again on August 30 with 2,332 passengers. This would be her last departure from the port for six years.

As the *Queen* approached New York, news arrived that war had been officially declared on Sunday, September 3, 1939. She had sailed with extra life rafts on board and with sealed Admiralty orders.

On arriving at Pier 90 on Monday, September 4, the *Mary* berthed and immediately was laid up. Many of her crew returned home on other Cunard ships, as the *Queen* was too valuable, too big a target for the Luftwaffe, for her to return to Southampton. Basically, no one knew what to do with her. Eventually, orders were received to paint the exterior of the ship in a drab gray, her ports and windows already having been so painted on her last trip.

Voices in Parliament were critical of the *Mary* and her sistership then nearing completion on the Clyde. "Too big and too costly to be risked" was typical of the tirades raised against the ships, but the critics soon would be proven very wrong.

At 8 p.m. on March 1, 1940, the Cunard White Star Line received a surprise telephone call from the Ministry of Shipping, which wanted their ship! The *Queen Mary* had been called up!

Six days later, the citizens of New York also had a surprise, for there, sailing up the Hudson River for the first time, was the newest, largest liner in the world, the *Queen Elizabeth*. The *Queen Mary* was already docked with the *Normandie* in New York Harbor, and now the *Queen Elizabeth* joined them — three of the world's greatest ocean liners berthed side by side. For two weeks they remained there, until, on March 21, the *Mary* sailed for Sydney, Australia. She stayed there for two weeks being partially fitted out as a troopship, including having extra kitchen, stores, and sanitary arrangements fitted. Most of her furnishings were put ashore for safekeeping.

After the Japanese attack on Pearl Harbor on December 7, 1941, Australia was in danger of invasion, and because most of the Australian troops were in England or Africa, American soldiers were needed quickly to defend Australia. Leaving the Indian Ocean, the *Queen Mary* went to New York, arriving on January 12, 1942. Twenty-five days were spent upgrading the troopship's capacity to 8,500. Standee bunks, some five deep, were fitted wherever there was space, and more armament, stores, and even more showers were fitted.

After loading 8,398 troops at night, she sailed on February 18 for Sydney. The ship had been built for the North Atlantic, so she had never been air-conditioned — a situation that created extreme discomfort, and even death in a few cases. In the meantime, it was reported that Hitler had promised a financial reward and the Iron Cross to the person who could sink either the *Queen Mary* or the *Queen Elizabeth*.

When the *Queen Mary* arrived back in New York on May 7, she received orders to revert back to her natural environment — the North Atlantic — to begin the famous "GI shuttle."

Reinforcements were urgently needed in Europe, and the *Mary* sailed after taking on 9,880 troops (with 875 crew, this was the first time a ship had ever sailed with more than 10,000 people aboard), who embarked on May 10. She steamed at 25.5 knots to Gourock, Scotland. After being ordered to Egypt with 9,357 troops — which resulted in more deaths from heat exhaustion in the Red Sea region — she returned to New York carrying German prisoners of war.

On August 2, the *Queen Mary* sailed with the incredible total of 15,125 troops (and 863 crew) — almost 16,000 people on one ship. Reaching Gourock on August 7, 1942, the liner reported a narrowly missed explosion — explained by the likelihood that an acoustic mine was detonated just as the *Mary* zigzagged along her course (a procedure that she used throughout the war to confuse submarines).

(Top) First-class smoking room on the Queen Mary. *(Bottom) Another of the beautiful public rooms on the* Queen.

Three great liners overlook the New York freeway, mothballed and awaiting call-up. Left to right: Normandie, Queen Mary, Queen Elizabeth. *Both the* Normandie *and the* Queen Elizabeth *later burned — the* Normandie *in New York and the* Elizabeth *in Hong Kong.*

On October 2, 1942, during one of these high-speed GI shuttle dashes across the Atlantic, a cruiser would always meet the *Queen* off the northern coast of Ireland to escort her through potentially dangerous waters to Scotland. The escorting cruiser would act as an antiaircraft defense ship, and six destroyers would provide antisubmarine cover.

On October 2, HMS Curaçao, the 4,200-ton cruiser that had been sent as escort vessel, saw the smoke of the Mary appear above the horizon, so the *Curaçao* turned about and started at full speed toward the British coast, knowing that the *Mary* would soon catch up to her and overtake her. The two ships met off the part of the northern Irish coast known, appropriately, as Bloody Foreland.

The *Queen Mary* maintained her zigzag course. A "figure-eight" zigzag was being used, which involved four minutes steaming on a mean (straight) course, then a 25-degree turn to starboard for eight minutes, 50-degree turn to port for eight minutes, and then a 25-degree turn back to her mean course. The *Curaçao* moved in rather close, and witnesses later said that an officer on the bridge was taking photographs of the *Queen* and was told, "You'll never get a better picture!"

What happened next has long been a matter of debate. The *Curaçao* should have been watching the *Mary* carefully, but somehow she had maneuvered in too close to the *Mary's* starboard side. Then, either a wrong helm order or — as was suggested later by testing-tank experiments — the interaction between the two vessels pulled the cruiser in front of the oncoming knife edge of the *Queen Mary's* bow.

People aboard the *Queen* felt either nothing or a slight jolt — or they believed they were being bombed as the liner's bow sliced through the cruiser at 28 1/2 knots. The time was 2:10 p.m.

During the awful brief moments that followed, the cruiser's stern section sank quickly, followed a few minutes later by the bow. The disaster claimed the lives of 331 officers and men; only 101 survived the calamity.

Despite the anguish felt by those who witnessed the event from aboard the *Queen Mary*, the liner could not stop. She could not risk the lives of 15,000 people by attempting a rescue in waters known to be frequented by U-boats. Stopping could easily have courted a greater catastrophe.

As the *Queen's* mighty bulk steamed through the wreckage of ship and men, horrified troops on the liner's decks threw life jackets overboard in a desperate attempt to aid survivors. The *Queen* immediately notified the escort destroyers, which sped to rescue the seamen thrashing about in the oily water.

The liner safely made Gourock, Scotland, where her crumpled bow was temporarily patched up with cement. Then she returned to the United States at a reduced speed of 24 knots and headed for drydock in Boston, where a new stem section had been constructed from templates rushed over from Britain.

From June 1943 to August 1944, the *Queen Mary* did a complete series of trooping voyages from New York (except for one from Halifax, Nova Scotia) to Britain. The troops always embarked at night — a procedure they had practiced earlier on full-size mock-ups of the ship at Camp Kilmer, so each man knew where to go and what to do when he arrived on board. The ship was also divided into "red," "white," and "blue" sections, and a soldier would be punished with extra duties if he trespassed into the wrong section.

Leaving New York with thousands of men on board, the *Mary* was in particular peril. With the additional weight of all her human cargo, she drew an extra two feet of water, so the men were ordered to stand still in their quarters while the ship left harbor. If they had rushed to one side of the boat to wave farewell to the Statue of Liberty, then the ship would have listed at least ten degrees and would have increased her draft on the "deep" side by four feet. This could have been enough to rupture the automobile and train tunnels beneath the Hudson River.

During the passages aboard the *Queen Mary,* the troops indulged in several activities that were not to Cunard's or the authorities' liking. Among these were dice games ("craps" was a great favorite). As far as the ship's crew members were concerned, gum chewing was unpopular (because it was difficult to clean off bulkheads and decks), as was the carving of initials in the teakwood handrails. The latter eventually was tolerated, and, as Captain Bisset later wrote, ". . . I decided not to make a fuss about this. These men might soon be going into battle, and some of them would never return to their homes and loved ones. Let them amuse themselves!" These carvings would later become treasured relics.

Thus the background of the *Queen Mary,* the "Gray Ghost" of World War II. Oddly enough, not only was the famed liner known as the Gray Ghost, but she ended up transporting a division that would soon be known as the "Phantom Nine" — a division that also would take its place in history.

Queen Mary *in war service. Escort blimp overhead.*

Five

The "Gray Ghost"

The latrine rumors were running rampant at Camp Kilmer, New Jersey, and the liveliest one was that we would be sailing to Europe on the *Queen Mary*. I didn't dare hope that this would be true, as I had been aboard this elegant ship during peaceful times to bid farewell to my aunt, now Mrs. James H. Crawford, when she traveled to Europe. I had accompanied my mother and my grandmother to see my aunt embark on this fantastic ship. My only thoughts, at that time, had been how I could get a job aboard the *Queen Mary*. Of course, all of the employees were British, so that was out of the question. I never dreamed that I would sail on that ship later, but I well remembered the luxurious accommodations and beautiful dining room, the swimming pools, and all the other great amenities of this luxury liner. As I remember, the *Queen* was more than a thousand feet long — or, to a golfer, it would be the length of a 340-yard hole.

At Camp Kilmer, we were given briefings on behavior in a friendly foreign country. We were also issued A Short Guide to Great Britain, which had been printed by the War Department. The book made a great effort to point out to us that the British had been at war since 1939, and it wasn't only the military who were involved, but men, women, children, and their homes. The Germans had tried to bomb the British into submission. The book stressed that we were guests of the British and we should do our best to act like guests. When I arrived there later, what amazed me was the calm acceptance by all of the British people of their fate in this war.

Finally, we received orders to load up on the troop trains that would take us to the ferry on the New Jersey side of the Hudson River. We left the troop train and marched onto the ferry for the ride across the river. If I remember correctly, it was after dark. On the other side, the ferry pulled up at the end of one of the huge piers, where we disembarked. As we entered the giant steel building, a black brass band was playing "Hold That Tiger" (the German tank was a Tiger tank), and the sound in that building was deafening. Lugging our equipment was a little ungainly, as we were wearing our steel helmets and carrying our carbines, bedrolls, gas masks, and duffel bags. We went up the gangplank one at a time, and

Antiaircraft gun crews practice emergency procedures.

I can remember looking down to the water and wondering how many feet the drop would be. I would judge that the first open deck was about fifty feet or more to the water. Except for the size, I had a real problem recognizing this as the same ship I had been aboard a few years earlier.

Everything was well organized, and we were given our deck and stateroom assignments right away. When some of us got to the stateroom, we found out that thirty of us would be occupying the fifteen bunks. Half of us were issued white buttons, which we had to wear, and the other half were given red buttons. We were told that we would be called to mess by the color of the button, and we would also have sleeping assignments according to button color: one night in the stateroom and one night on deck. I found it hard to believe that this ship was the *Queen Mary*. When I finally was able to move around the ship a bit, I located the main stairway, and at its head was a painting of Queen Mary — the only thing left on that ship from the original luxury liner. The swimming pool had been converted to a dining room — and not a luxury one, either. Tables were bolted to the floor so that each of us could stand and enjoy our meals from our mess kits. There were no chairs.

How many of us were aboard was a secret, but we estimated that there had to be about 15,000. There were a little more than 10,000 in our division, plus a tank destroyer battalion, an Australian battalion, a Red Cross battalion, a WAC battalion, and sundry other outfits. After coming up with the estimate of about 15,000 (plus the crew of about a thousand), I walked around the deck and counted the life rafts that were piled and strapped on the deck. There were about a hundred of these, which held twenty persons each. It didn't take a genius to figure out that it would be a long swim for about 12,000 of us if that ship were torpedoed. I was not allowed up on the boat deck, so I did not see the lifeboats, which probably would have handled another thousand or so.

On August 20, 1944, we sailed out of New York Harbor. The *Queen Mary* traveled alone, because there was nothing afloat that could catch her. Reports were that she traveled at about thirty knots. We were told that it took a submarine twenty minutes to sight a torpedo, so we could feel the ship lean every fifteen minutes as the course was changed. The sea was like glass all the way across, and we had no encounters with stormy weather.

Each of us was issued one of those inflatable life preservers to wear around our waists, and we were ordered to wear them at all times. They had two little gas cylinders that would inflate the belt when activated. Every now and then, one of the fellows would accidentally (or otherwise) inflate the life belt and have to get a replacement cylinder.

Before departure, an announcement came that our field artillery would man all of the guns on the ship. Most of the guns were antiaircraft along the upper decks, except that a six-inch gun was on the stern with a number of other weapons. It was generally conceded that if anything happened, the *Queen* would be running, so it was best to have the big guns in the stern. We were then told that all of us would be on submarine watch during daylight hours.

Being on submarine watch was interesting and boring. I didn't have any idea what I was supposed to be looking for. I had seen motion pictures of submarines, but it was much different being on a deck fifty or sixty feet above the water and looking out into a vast sea.

When the ship cleared the harbor, our field artillery immediately began firing practice with all the guns on board. Rumors had it that enemy submarine packs were operating in the North Atlantic, so our course was more southerly. Once, a general alarm was sounded suddenly when five submarines were sighted off the starboard bow. When the "submarines" started to spout water and were identified as whales, the all-clear came through. We experienced two more general alarms on that

The "Gray Ghost" dwarfs her supply ships in port.

voyage: once when an aircraft flew over at very high altitude and the other when we sighted a life raft.

We knew that every effort was being made to protect the *Queen Mary* and her passengers, but we were not aware of the specifics. Unbeknownst to us, a blimp flew over the area from New York City — until we were about 300 miles out. The blimp flew about 300 feet above the sea, trying to ferret out U-boats and "wolf packs" lurking in the area. It would fly at a ground speed of about sixty miles per hour and would scan the sea electronically in front of the ship it was escorting. If the blimp's electronics detected metal, the crew would check for shipwrecks, check for friendly submarines, and then report the incident to a fleet of destroyers and to fixed-wing aircraft. They also would try to ascertain and report the direction in which the submarine was traveling. Then they would circle out farther in an attempt to identify other members of the wolf pack — if indeed there were more in the area.

The first night out, I was chosen to sleep in the stateroom, and I decided that if there was any way for me to arrange it, I would not sleep there again. The porthole was sealed, and fifteen bunks were jammed in that stateroom — three rows, five high. Besides the fifteen bunks, there was all the equipment that each man had brought on board — helmets,

An impressive view of the Queen Mary *traveling alone and at speed.*

duffel bags, rifles, gas masks, and bedrolls for thirty of us. The stateroom may have been a reasonable size for two people, but with fifteen bunks and the gear belonging to thirty men, there was no room left. There was little or no air, and every time you would try to roll over, you bumped into someone either above or below you. It was a torture rack. The second night, I was all right because I was due to sleep on deck, but then I called for playing cards to see who would win what color button on a certain day. My luck was with me, because I slept on deck the rest of the way. Since the nights were clear and warm, this was really delightful, except for the hardness of the deck.

One day when I was stretched out on deck, I felt a boot in the seat of the pants. An officer was standing there with one of the Red Cross girls, and he said, "Sit up, we are going to sing." I had been taught very well by my NCOs, so I immediately responded, "Is that an order, sir?" He decided he had better move farther down the deck if he wanted to show off in front of that girl. I didn't hear any singing from down there, either, so his reception must have been pretty cool there, also.

For exercise, we would walk around the ship, a pretty good distance. We entertained ourselves by playing cribbage or poker or by shooting dice during the whole trip. With the ship as jammed as it was, there was

The Queen Mary *at anchor in the Firth of Clyde off Gourock, Scotland. Here troops disembarked into ferries and pleasure steamers for transfer to shore bases.*

no way to have organized activities. The wide promenade deck was always covered with men playing cards, leaning over the rail looking at the sea, sleeping, or just wandering around. After almost six days, we were delighted to get where we were going. We were beginning to feel a little stir-crazy.

Needless to say, there were no lounge chairs or any of the fancy amenities of the former luxury liner. This ship had been stripped to the bare necessities to carry the maximum number of troops. The teakwood railing (I thought it was mahogany) of the promenade deck was about twelve inches wide on the top, and the men all took turns carving their initials into it. We had three meals a day, and much of the day was spent in line for breakfast, in line to wash the mess kit, in line for lunch, in line to wash the mess kit, in line for dinner, and in line one last time to wash the mess kit. I certainly don't recall any cocktail hour before dinner.

After a few days, we sighted the Azores in the distance — the only land we saw during the whole passage. Near the Azores, a general alarm was sounded when someone spotted a life raft floating off the port bow. We could feel the power surge of the engines as the captain apparently ordered full speed. We passed that raft, but no one was in it. We were told that the *Queen* would not have stopped to pick up survivors even if there were any, because enemy submarine commanders had used this type of trick to lure ships to be torpedoed. Submarine activity was still being reported north of us.

The sixth morning, there was dense fog, and I leaned over the rail looking down at the water. Suddenly I saw a man in a rowboat. My first thought was, "What in hell is he doing way out here?" But it developed that the *Queen* had arrived during the night in the Firth of Clyde, Scotland, and had anchored. The dense fog kept us from seeing land. There were no deepwater docks, so we had to disembark from our anchorage in the bay.

The trip across had been as smooth as glass, and I hadn't even had a qualm of seasickness (although one of our fellows never left the stateroom from the time the ship departed until it arrived in Scotland). Historical information says that there wasn't a GI who wouldn't remember the severe rolling of the *Queen Mary*. I can honestly say that our trip was so smooth that I don't remember the ship rolling at all. The only time we felt anything was when the ship zigzagged. The trip took five days, sixteen hours, and six minutes to cover 3,615 miles at an average speed of 26.56 knots. Despite the beautiful weather — or because of it — this was one of the longest trips the *Queen* made between New York and Scotland — normally a distance of 3,000 miles.

We were ordered to pick up our gear and follow the line down into the bowels of the ship, where there was a very narrow steel staircase (gangway) that wound down and down and down. It had to be six or eight stories from our deck to the water level, and just managing to carry all of our equipment on that narrow iron staircase was a major feat. We finally came out about ten feet above the water, where there was a huge cargo door opening with a plank between the *Queen* and a ferry. Sailors were lined along the opening with boathooks and we were told to walk the plank. It was a slightly hairy experience doing a balancing act with my helmet, gas mask, carbine, bedroll, and duffel bag and then walking that plank for about ten feet, or farther, to the ferry. I don't know whether or not anyone fell into the water, but the sailors were there with their boathooks if they did.

The history of the *Queen Mary* details the round trips from Gourock, Scotland, to New York. I had never heard of Gourock, Scotland, until I read the history. As far as all of us were concerned, the *Queen* had landed in Greenock, not Gourock.

The *Queen*'s history also details the fact that she carried three quarters of a million troops during the war. It appears from the research that she transported approximately 380,000 of the ground fighting troops to the

European theater of operations (ETO) in thirty-one voyages —
somewhere between 25 and 50 percent of the ground forces. The navy
and the air force would have transported most of their own troops, so the
impact of the *Queen Mary* on the war effort was considerable. Since there
were slightly more than three million military personnel in the European
theater, including army air forces and navy, it's no wonder that Adolf
Hitler put such a high price on the sinking of the *Queen*. Naturally, there
are many of us grateful that he failed in that, as in many of his other
ventures.

The ferry took us to Greenock, Scotland, where we immediately
boarded trains for Tidworth Barracks, near Salisbury, England. That train
ride was memorable to me for one incident. A young conductor about
twenty-five years of age was on that train, and one of our fellows asked
him in a very insulting way why he wasn't in the service. He replied, "I
bought mine at Dunkirk and am no longer fit for active duty."
("Dunkirk" was an all-out effort to evacuate allied troops retreating from
the Germans from the continent to England.) There was no further
comment along those lines.

The trip to Tidworth Barracks was very smooth and without incident.
For most of us, this was the first time in a foreign country. The thatch-
roofed homes in England were a real curiosity, and we were very
interested in everything going on around us.

Changing of the Guard at Buckingham Palace, London. Front row (third and fourth from left), Knachel and McAvoy, and (seventh and eighth from left), McWhirter and Waterman. Note that most in the crowd are GIs, even at the fence.

Six

England

We arrived at Tidworth Barracks, a British army base, where we would draw all of our equipment for the trip across the English Channel. The war had progressed to where the Germans had been driven back pretty much to their own border. Our training now was in identification of enemy soldiers in the field. We were taken to a field area and asked to identify any enemy that we could see. I didn't see any of them, even though they were standing in the open about a hundred to two hundred yards away, blending into the background. I decided immediately that the army would be better off sending me right home. I was about the poorest one in aircraft identification, and now I couldn't even see an enemy in the open. It was rather sobering.

We were then given practice in the timing of tossing hand grenades so that the enemy wouldn't have time to throw them back. We also were given lessons in other explosives, such as primer cord. At the same time, we were trained how to destroy our vehicle in case of imminent capture: one grenade on top of the gas tank, one grenade in the code machine, and one in the radio set.

We were awarded the European, African, Middle Eastern Theater Campaign Medal at this time for our participation in events in the area. We also were given passes to enjoy the countryside, and we did get to Salisbury a couple of times. Then we were given forty-eight hours in London, and what a delight that was. We toured London like any other sightseers and enjoyed Madame Tussaud's Wax Museum, the Tower of London, Buckingham Palace, Westminster Abbey, 10 Downing Street, and Piccadilly Circus. Just as it had gotten dark, two of us were walking down the street when the air-raid sirens sounded. Two young girls were approaching us, about ten years of age, and one stepped up to me and asked, "Aye saye, what time is it?" I told her it was 9:15, and she turned to her friend and calmly said, "Aye saye, they're early tonight."

At the time the sirens went off, I thought to myself, uh-oh, this is it. The young girls changed my attitude, and I watched the casual manner the British people adopted as they moved slowly but deliberately to the bomb shelters. We followed them down into a shelter that held hundreds of people. After we felt the shocks of the bombing, the all-

Ten Downing Street, where passes must be shown.

Posting of the guard at the Court of St. James.

Changing of the Guard in battle dress. Red coats were not worn during the war.

clear was sounded, and everyone casually went back to whatever they had been doing.

We watched the changing of the guard at Buckingham Palace, but the guards wore battle gear instead of the traditional red coats. As we stood watching, a tourist guide came along and spoke to the crowd, telling interesting stories about the royal family. He then said, "Do you see that open window on the top floor? That is the room that Eleanor Roosevelt stayed in when she was here. We are still airing it out." The guide was dressed like Winston Churchill.

There were specific places in London where military personnel could go for meals, so we went to one of them, since rationing was severe in England. When we had finished, we were each given a navel orange — as nice an orange as I can remember. As we walked out onto the street with our oranges in hand, a woman was approaching us with a cute little girl, about two or three years old. On impulse, I reached out and handed the orange to the child. She shied away from it, and her mother said, "She doesn't know what it is — she has never seen one." Due to the rationing, oranges were not available. My buddy and I both gave the little girl our oranges so that she could enjoy at least two of them. On the black market, those oranges probably were worth about $20 each.

In Piccadilly Circus, we were amazed at the brazen manner of the prostitutes. American servicemen evidently were fair game, and they aggressively pushed their wares, even suggesting a quickie in a taxicab. Apparently this was legal under British law. One Irish girl was pushing the fact that an Irish girl was much warmer than an English one. It was shocking, even to me, despite the fact that I was not unfamiliar with prostitutes trying to operate in the hotels at night back in the States.

A group of us went to the wax museum, where the realism of those figures was amazing — so much so that one of our fellows turned to a bobby standing by the door and asked him a question — only to find out that the bobby was wax. The museum had life-size figures of all the principals in the war: Hitler, Mussolini, Hirohito, Roosevelt, Churchill, and Stalin.

Upon returning to the base, we were ordered to start stowing supplies in our half-track vehicle. Our crew was inside the vehicle and trucks would pull alongside and hand over what we would need. It started with thirty 500-pound land mines, which we stowed — fifteen on each side — in the racks on the outside of the half-track. Then we were issued thirty hand-grenade-size detonators for those mines. We left those in the case. Then cans of machine-gun ammunition were handed into the vehicle — 7,500 rounds. Next came the bazooka, with ten shells, followed by a case of twenty-four hand grenades and a half-dozen rifle grenades. We were each issued 120 rounds of personal ammunition for our carbines, to be carried on us. Following a practice already in effect, we each placed a clip of fifteen rounds in the carbine and attached to the gun stock a pocket containing two clips. The driver was issued 450 rounds of .45-caliber ammunition for his "grease gun" (the name that had been given to the metal tommy gun).

Just then a fellow came along tossing a foot-square box into each vehicle. I caught our box, which was very light, and asked what it was. He just laughed. So I opened the box and found a thousand condoms. Until this point, I hadn't realized that this was all-out war. Those condoms became invaluable to us in a way the manufacturer had never intended. A tank division raises a tremendous amount of dust and dirt, and we found that a condom fit perfectly over the muzzle of the machine gun. Contrary to the manufacturer's claims, we could shoot right through it, but it did keep the barrel clean.

We were also issued a strange contraption that was attached to our radio set with an electric eye — a new invention they wanted us to try out. It allowed transmission of a signature or written message over the airwaves at a distance of up to forty-five miles. That invention was a huge success, but not with us. It required very fine tuning, and we had trouble keeping it in tune. I don't know why they decided to put it in vehicles that had as rough a ride as ours, but it wasn't long before they took them back out.

We moved out of Tidworth Barracks to Bournemouth, where we drove onto the LSTs (Landing Ship, Tank). I pity the poor sailors who served on those flat-bottomed ships, because, in my opinion, that had to be the worst sea duty any sailor could draw. The ride in those ships was a rough one.

I had to go to the bathroom when we were at the docks, so I headed into the head — or perch, latrine, or whatever — to take care of myself. While in there, I looked up on the wall, where some GI before me had written a poem that has stuck in my mind all these years:

Someone has pulled a dirty caper
And left me here without any paper.
My boat is due and I cannot linger
Look out, rear end, here comes my finger.

Early in the morning, we sailed out of Bournemouth into the English Channel, and even though it was partly sunny, the water was extremely choppy. The LST rode those waves, hitting each one violently as the ship gradually settled down to a wallow. Then it would rise up again and bounce along the waves until it wallowed again. There were some Jeeps chained to the deck, and they rode up on their chains when the ship would roll. I wondered what kept the ship herself from rolling over. Our half-track was down in the hold, so we went down and played poker for a while until I began to feel a little queasy. I decided I had better get up in the air and walk around the ship to try to duck what I felt was coming. I was doing fine until I walked by an open door and got a strong whiff of the engine room below. I just made it to the rail.

After relieving myself, I looked up and saw five of the navy crew doing the same thing I had done. I decided that the best solution for me would be to get to the center of the ship, where there was the least motion, and try to get some sleep. When I woke up, I moved very slowly but felt pretty good. Then I realized that the water was much calmer and the ship wasn't bouncing around. We were now in the bay approaching Omaha Beach in Normandy, France.

The LST rammed straight ahead into the beach, and I went down to my vehicle. I then walked to the front of the LST, where they had opened the huge front area. A leadline dropped down from the ship showed that we were in fifteen feet of water. I walked back to my vehicle and told the bunch that it looked as if we would have to wait for the tide to go out before we could get off this tub. But just then I heard the order to wind up the motors and move out. I couldn't believe it. The vehicles immediately began to leave the ship. We were quite far toward the rear, and when it came our turn, we moved right off onto a sand ramp that had been put there by these seagoing bulldozers.

Seven

Normandy, France, and Luxembourg

We moved to a bivouac area near where we had landed in Normandy, then immediately set up our pup tents in the standard manner, digging a little drainage ditch around the tent. It was a decent day when we arrived, but the following day it started to rain, and kept raining for at least a week. Doesn't it always rain in the service? Finally, the ditch around the tent no longer carried off the water. Now it was seeping up through the ground. Our bedrolls were dank and musty, and we were miserable. After a week of rain, the sun came out, and soon the whole area looked like some kind of flea market. Anything that would hold something off the ground and in the sun was draped with blankets, bedrolls, clothing, etc. That night, it was terrific to sleep in a clean-smelling bedroll. We had even struck our tents so that the sun could dry out the ground.

One morning, we were called together in company formation and the captain advised us that saluting would no longer be necessary. We would be moving up shortly and officers still would be entitled to the respect of an officer, but for the safety of all concerned, saluting would not be observed. We bandied that one around in good shape and chuckled over the fact that it was beginning to look like the officers wanted to be on our side for a change.

I went to the major and suggested to him that we needed a trailer to carry our bedrolls, etc. I came up with this idea because there was a motor pool on the beach with about 500 trailers waiting to be requisitioned, and the work area inside our half-track was very limited. The major said that our table of organization did not authorize us to have a trailer, and the only way to amend the table of organization was to make a formal approach to the Pentagon in Washington. He figured that approval of that request probably would take until sometime into the next century. I told him I felt a midnight requisition (in plain words, theft) would be the way to go. So we set up a beautiful plan. We arranged for one of the fellows to engage the guard in conversation while two other fellows with a Jeep took a trailer from the far end of the motor pool. It worked beautifully, and as soon as we got the trailer back to the bivouac, we repainted it, put a set of bogus numbers on it, and then threw mud all over it.

A day or two later, I saw an MP captain and two MPs minutely studying the trailer. When I asked them what they were doing, the captain placed me under arrest for stealing the trailer. He took me to the major, who did a fantastic job of acting. The major blew his top and told the captain to leave me with him because he was fed up with my antics and would take care of me. The captain agreed. As soon as he was gone, I said, "Let's wait until we get orders to move, and I will go back and get it." The major agreed with the plan, but he decided that he would have someone else do it instead of me to prevent a problem in case it didn't work out. Needless to say, we left the Cherbourg Peninsula pulling that trailer.

The next eight days would be as memorable as any of my days in the service. We traveled across France to a heroes' welcome in every city, town, and hamlet. Here was the armored might of the United States Army on display, and the French people were overjoyed to see it. After five years of brutal occupation by the Germans, their fear was still widespread, so our arrival was a great relief.

As we moved toward the German border, our route took us through Paris, where the streets were lined with people cheering, even though it was raining. Every window was overflowing with people waving and throwing flowers to us. We were traveling at a pretty good speed when we arrived at the Place de la Concorde, where we had to make a left turn. The half-track skidded sideways on the cobblestones, and I thought that we were going over, but we didn't.

The tumultuous welcome continued all the way through France. Some people tossed us eggs and flowers. One woman tossed me an egg as we went rolling by, but I missed it. Needless to say, that meant we had a bit of a mess to clean up in the vehicle. From time to time, we would notice women with quizzical expressions staring at the end of our machine gun. Just beyond Paris, we stopped overnight in a town called Clichy-sur-Bois.

The triumphal march across France was a great social event everywhere we went. It was almost embarrassing, because we were receiving all the praise earned by the men who had gone before us. One man ran toward me and threw his arms around me in greeting. He had a fair amount of stubble on his face, and, to my surprise, he kissed me on the mouth. It was the most unpleasant experience I can remember. The welcome that we received was enormously exhilarating, but we would soon earn all those flowers, kisses, and greetings.

We had been traveling without stopping for a long period when we finally arrived in the city of Longwy, on the Luxembourg-Belgian border,

Welcome to the liberators.   *Bob Fulton in Lintgen, Luxembourg.*

where we all pulled up in the middle of the city for a rest stop. It is a little embarrassing to have to go in no uncertain terms and not have a private place to do it. The people swarmed around, greeting us, while we were all bouncing from one foot to the other. Finally, one of the fellows tried to get through to them that we needed a bathroom. It was a real problem trying to make them understand, because we used the word bathroom and they kept wondering why we wanted to take a bath. The commander of our column must have found a good bar, because he sure didn't worry about the rest of us.

We entered the Grand Duchy of Luxembourg and almost immediately were in Luxembourg City. Once again, the welcome was terrific. There were people in every window and lining the streets, throwing flowers and cheering as we went by. We continued on through Lintgen, Luxembourg, where a welcoming arch had been erected. Finally we reached our destination, the small town of Schoenfels, where we were billeted in a castle. Schoenfels is in the Valley of the Seven Castles, and we were in one of them. The area was much like New Hampshire — hilly and tree-covered and beautiful. There was no furniture in the castle, which formerly had been used by the Germans. In fact, German pinup pictures of rugged-looking naked women were still on the walls. We

Schoenfels Castle, Grand Duchy of Luxembourg.

Schoenfels Castle, our home for two months.

settled into the castle and Schoenfels for the next couple of months.

Not long after arriving in Luxembourg, the quality of our food began to deteriorate. In the beginning, we had fresh food, but gradually there was less and less of it, and we were being fed C-rations and K-rations most of the time. There were small deer in the woods nearby, so we started to hunt for our own fresh meat. We did not realize it at the time, but doing this led to a solution of our problem. We didn't know that the mess was required to report how many men ate each meal there, and as the numbers at meals decreased, the inspector general became curious. The next thing we knew, we were being questioned about our eating habits, and we told the men frankly that we were getting our own food. We found out that fresh food had been allotted to us, but we had not been getting it.

The "Red Ball Express" was the nickname we had given to the quartermaster unit that trucked supplies from the various ports to the front. The drivers of these trucks suddenly found that they were carrying very valuable black-market goods, and a fortune could be made that way. Can you imagine having a truckload of fresh meat and driving the truck through Paris? Most of the trucks were not making it to their destinations

Town of Schoenfels, castle in background. (Right) Bud Knachel on the roof of the castle.

because the temptations were too great. It didn't matter whether the truck was carrying cigarettes, candy, fresh meat, fresh food, or whatever. There was a ready market for anything that was on board.

The inspector general's investigation suddenly brought all of this into the open, and once again we were getting fresh food. The U.S. Army realized then that it had to have a system of checks and balances to ensure the delivery of those supplies. In any war area, the black market will operate with anything that it can get.

Three of us became acquainted with the Strauss family in Schoenfels: a man, his wife, a son fourteen years of age, and a daughter eight years old. The son was totally enthralled with the American army. One day, Mr. Strauss asked us if we would do him the honor of attending a very special event at his home. We accepted. It developed that the butcher was coming to town, and Mr. Strauss had a large pig that he wanted butchered — a great event in these small towns. The butcher arrived with a horse and wagon, and in the wagon he had what appeared to be a wooden boat that could be tilted up from either end. He maneuvered the pig into the boat, after which he picked up two mallets, one with a huge spike hanging loosely from the center of it. He placed this in the middle of the pig's head and with the other mallet drove the nail into the pig's brain, killing it instantly. The butcher immediately reached under and cut the pig's throat, and the blood spurted out into the boat. Then he lifted up one end of the boat to drain the blood into pails. Next he proceeded to clean the hair from the pig and to dress it down. Since I hadn't come from a farm family, I can't say I was totally enthralled with this whole performance.

Thanksgiving was approaching, and the army encouraged the local people to invite us to enjoy Thanksgiving dinner with them. The Strauss

Pinups on the wall of Schoenfels Castle. Lower left picture left by the Germans.

family immediately invited the three of us (one of the other two spoke German) to join them, and we accepted appreciatively. As long as I live, I will never forget that dinner. First of all, we entered the home fully armed, as usual, and stacked our rifles against the wall in the dining room. I then took off my helmet and placed it next to the rifles, with the liner facing up. When I noticed Mrs. Strauss staring down into my helmet, I realized that she was looking at the toilet paper that we usually carried under the straps of our helmets. At the time I thought, oh well, you can't win them all. Little did I know. When we were seated at the table, Mr. Strauss told us he knew two American songs. Since none of the family could speak English, we knew that one of the songs would be "It's a Long Way to Tipperary," which none of us happened to know. He sang verse after verse of it, and we hummed along with him, although he seemed slightly puzzled that we had not joined in. Then he was asked what the other song was. He told us that the 5th Infantry Division had occupied Luxembourg during World War I, when he was a boy, and they had taught him this song. He immediately broke into a lusty version of "No Balls At All," singing one verse after another without the faintest idea what the words meant. I didn't dare look at my buddies, so the whole time he was singing, I was looking at the ceiling, the floor, the walls, anyplace but at them. Finally, the song ended, and I have very little memory of the dinner after that. They were wonderful people, the Strausses, and very nice to us.

An American civilian who had been living in Luxembourg reported to us that there were spies in the area, and he filed a complaint against some people who lived a short distance from the castle. We reported this to headquarters, and we were soon advised not to pay any attention to this guy, as he was attempting to use us for his own benefit. He was told in no uncertain terms what we thought of that.

Marlene Dietrich came to a theater in Mersch to entertain, and many of us went to the show. We remarked at the time that she had guts to be in that area, so close to the Germans, since she had been a German citizen herself, and Adolf Hitler would not have appreciated her entertaining us.

At one point, my mother was having some difficulties at home, and I wanted to talk to the Red Cross about their checking on her, so I asked for a pass to go back to Bastogne where the Red Cross office was located. I got a ride with the regular messenger going to Bastogne and arrived there only to find that the Red Cross representative was in Paris for a few days. I had made the trip for nothing. (Travel in a war zone is never easy.) A few weeks later, I again asked for permission to go to Bastogne and again rode with the messenger. When I walked into the Red Cross office and asked for the representative, I was told he was in Paris. So I blew my stack with a few unkind remarks. Then the officer who was there said, "Maybe I can help you, sergeant." It was at that point that I noticed he had a cross on his collar, indicating he was a clergyman. I apologized for my remarks and told him my problem. He promised to take care of it, which he did.

On Sundays, a member of the clergy would come to our bivouac area to hold services. He would carry with him a folding altar that looked much like a paperhanger's folding table. He would announce that the Catholic mass would be held at 9, the Jewish service at 10, and the Protestant service at 11. The same clergyman would hold all three services at the aforementioned times. My background had always been that I had to attend church every Sunday. The war changed that attitude. We understood that we should attend church whenever possible, but that God was available to us at all times.

During these days in Luxembourg, the allied air force would be delivering the great one thousand bomber strikes, and the planes would fly over us on their way into Germany. I can remember one beautiful, cloudless day when we began to hear the rumble of many motors. Looking up, we could see the squadrons of flying fortresses, thirty-three to a squadron, in V-formation. Those planes were minute in size from that distance, but each motor of the planes was trailing vapor. By the time squadron after squadron had passed over, the day was overcast. We remarked at the time that so many bombers surely meant somebody was catching hell.

On the enemy side of things, the Germans were moving ahead with rocketry, and every now and then we would hear a V-1 go over. I never did see one of these rockets, but it had a very distinctive noise that thumped along like a motor with a bad piston. Sometimes the motor would shut off, and then we would all hold our breaths and wait. The Germans fired those things by putting in a certain amount of fuel and letting it fly until it ran out. Then it would plunge to earth and explode. It was not accurate, but it did cause concern.

After our triumphal eight-day march across France, we took up positions all along the Luxembourg-Germany border. We would tune into the BBC (British Broadcasting Corporation) and listen to the news of the war for both Europe and the Far East. We could also tune into the German radio and listen to Axis Sally (Axis Sally was one of these American women traitors who seem to appear in every war), who would broadcast to the American troops. In her very sexy, sultry voice, she would talk to the American GIs, asking if they missed their wives and if they missed cuddling up to their wives at night. She also asked if the GIs wondered who was taking their places, cuddling up to their wives in their absence. We would all joke about it, but when one of our buddies received a "Dear John" letter, it would really hit home.

The reason we listened to Axis Sally was that the U.S. Air Force would complete a bombing mission over Germany and then, as the last matter of business, would drop a parachute with the latest hit records addressed to Axis Sally. They decided that if she was going to play records over the air, at least she should play the latest hits. She did play them, and we enjoyed them. She would also broadcast her thanks to the pilots for the records.

One night, we were listening to Axis Sally when suddenly she remarked that she wanted to welcome the 9th Armored Division to Luxembourg, and then she named the towns where we were located. Since we were on the secret list, this came as a bit of a shock. She then made the prophetic remark, "To you boys of the 9th Armored, I just want to say that we know you are there and we will be coming for you soon." At the time, we thought that it was funny. It probably was lucky that Axis Sally was not working in conjunction with German intelligence. She apparently had better sources about our positions than they did.

The only safety a messenger had was in speed, so it was not uncommon to meet a Jeep coming pell-mell. All of our drivers were taught that the less time you give a sniper, the better the chances for survival. One particular day, a Jeep with four men in it came around a bend in the road and found a farmer with a hay wagon blocking the way. The Jeep driver went off the side of the road and the vehicle turned over four times going down the slope. Each time it rolled, it ejected one man from the Jeep — until it finally came to rest on its four wheels. We raced to assist the men, and as we got to each one, he would sit up and say he was all right. What had really saved these fellows was the wire cutter on the front of the vehicle. The Germans had a practice of stringing piano wire across the road to try to catch a driver with his windshield down — and, in essence, to decapitate him. To prevent this, angle irons had been installed on the fronts of the Jeeps. The irons extended vertically to the height of the windshield and then extended forward at a forty-five-degree angle for about six inches. This bar would catch the piano wire and cut it. In this instance, however, the angle iron kept the Jeep from rolling over onto the men, even though it meant they were tossed out of the vehicle.

One of the most dangerous guns ever invented was the grease gun, or tommy gun. This was the all-metal submachine gun with a cover that folded over the top. The cover had a prong extending from it that was inserted into the bolt of the gun to keep it from firing — in other words, a safety. Unfortunately, this cover could be just slightly raised, giving the appearance of being safe, even though the prong might not be in the bolt. We had a number of incidents with this gun, and a couple of them come to mind. A messenger arrived in a Jeep, got out of the vehicle, reached back into the car, and grabbed his grease gun by the barrel. The gun fired. He was miraculously lucky: The bullet entered the sleeve of his field jacket at the wrist and exited at the elbow, without touching him.

The other incident was tragic, because it had to do with the little children who always flocked around us. We always enjoyed them tremendously. This particular day, a truck driver arrived and was stepping from the cab of the truck just as a little boy ran up to greet him. The gun fired, hitting the boy in the foot, and he was rushed to a hospital. In both cases, the drivers had the covers closed, but that little bit of difference between a cover that was fully shut or slightly ajar was critical. The grease gun seemed to be our mass-produced response to the German burp gun.

A collaborator, a big fellow, begged us for protection. He had cooperated with the Germans against his own people, and now he wanted us to save him from the wrath of the local citizens. Swastikas were drawn on the houses of people who had sold out to the Germans, so collaborators were easily recognized. We informed him that he had made his bed and he had to lie in it. We were not there to interfere in civilian life — it was none of our business.

During the night, we would set up outpost positions and post guards. We would also take some C-ration cans and string them together from tree to tree, about six inches from the ground. One night, the cans started rattling, and machine guns zeroed in. We opened fire and heard nothing

Collaborator's home.   Another collaborator.

further until morning, when we found that a deer had stumbled on our warning system. Most nights were pitch black, so it was impossible to see anything.

The main fighting of the war at this time was up north at Aachen, Germany, and our division had been spread loosely along a hundred miles of front, inside Luxembourg on the German border. It was apparent from all of the intelligence we were receiving that nothing was expected in front of us, and our field artillery was being rationed to a couple of rounds a day. Many times, targets would be passed up because they didn't want to use up their ammunition ration if a better target approached. There was absolutely no indication of anything to come. We were awarded the Rhineland Battle Star to the European, African, Middle Eastern Theater Campaign Ribbon.

A mine expert came to advise us on techniques for disarming German mines. A detail was sent to learn about this and have him explain the intricacies of the job. Unfortunately, he was not an expert in the particular mine that he demonstrated that day. It was a tragic affair.

At about this time, something happened that had many of us laughing but was causing major problems. The army would give the officers a monthly ration of liquor, but enlisted men were not entitled to

Jeep with wire cutter in front.

any. Suddenly we heard that someone had stolen the officers' ration of liquor, and a full investigation was ordered. We thought it was hilarious. Needless to say, this investigation did not have the sympathy of the enlisted men, although it was being pushed aggressively by the officers. But December 16, 1944, changed everything — including the demise of that investigation.

Lieutenant General Kinnard (Ret.), in the Bulge Bugle of February 1991, gave a very condensed synopsis of the Battle of the Bulge.

First, where did it take place? The German attack was along an eighty-five-mile front in the Ardennes sector of Belgium and Luxembourg, from Monschau in the north down through the Losheim Gap and Schnee Eiffel Mountains and then through the mountainous Ardennes Forest to Echternach.

Second, when did it happen? The Germans launched their attack at dawn on December 16, 1944, and the battle was essentially over by January 25, 1945.

Third, what did the opposing forces look like just prior to the battle? The U.S. forces were five-plus divisions very thinly holding this large sector, which was known as the "ghost front" because we were so thin on the ground. This sector had for some time been used as a rest area for war-weary veteran divisions and for newly arrived divisions to cut their combat teeth. The total strength of the U.S. forces in this sector on December 16 was about 75,000. As for the Germans, their strength was about 250,000, with almost 1,000 tanks and 1,900 artillery pieces. This formidable force comprised three armies totaling some thirty divisions.

Fourth, what was the genesis and overall objective of the German attack, and how did they manage to achieve such a complete surprise? This operation, which the Germans code-named "Christrose," was the brainchild of Adolf Hitler himself. Its objective was to capture the port city of Antwerp and destroy the allied forces north of a line Antwerp-Brussels-Bastogne. Hitler directed that the extensive planning for Christrose should begin in September of 1944, and he insisted on very thorough and highly secret preparations for, and execution of, the operation. Great attention was given to secrecy and deception. For example, certain key roads were covered with straw and hay to muffle the sound of their track vehicles as they moved to assembly areas for the attack. In spite of the elaborate precautions, however, there were a few American intelligence people who deduced that the Germans were planning an attack through the Ardennes. But these few were unable to convince their superiors — all of whom felt that the Germans were on the ropes and incapable of mounting a major offensive. So it is fair to say that the complete surprise the Germans achieved was a combination of their skillful planning and their cover of deception, accentuated by the complacency, self-delusion, and lack of imagination of allied commanders in general.

Fifth, what did the Germans accomplish? Their initial attacks were not only a surprise but also in such overwhelming strength that they quickly broke through the thin shell of U.S. forces and plunged westward, creating a very large salient (or bulge) in U.S. lines. Their deepest advance took them east of Rochefort, almost a hundred-mile advance from their starting positions.

Sixth, what finally stopped the German advance? There were several factors: The weather turned severely cold and snowy, and this presented a greater problem for the attackers than for the defenders. Also, the allied reaction was swift and massive, as forces were turned to strike the bulge from several directions, and units such as the 101st Airborne and 82nd Airborne Divisions were moved into blocking positions. Finally, there was gallantry, and the staying power of the forces that the Germans initially attacked. They fought bravely and skillfully as individuals and small groups, as well as in units of all sizes. It was very clear to these men that all the chips were down on this one, and that there could be only one winner.

Finally, what were the principal results of the Battle of the Bulge?
The total German casualties were about the same number as their initial
assault force — almost 250,000. The Germans also lost about 600 tanks
and about 1,600 airplanes. On the U.S. side, our total casualties were
about the same as the number initially manning the Ardennes sector —
about 75,000. But the really significant outcome of the Battle of the Bulge
was that it undoubtedly saved the allies a great many more casualties. If
the Germans had used the quarter of a million men they lost in the battle
to garrison their fortified positions protecting Germany, our losses
certainly would have been much greater.

Also in that same issue of the Bulge Bugle, Brigadier General Oliver
Patton stated, "Is it not strange we have come here today in memory of
the worst Christmas of our lives? A Christmas lost in the savagery of the
greatest battle ever fought by the United States Army.

"On this day forty-six years ago, the German army struck us by
surprise on a sixty-mile front from Monschau in Belgium to Echternach
in Luxembourg — a front thinly held by five American divisions, two
mechanized cavalry squadrons, and a battalion of armored infantry. The
center was smashed and overrun — the shoulders held by desperate
courage.

"Forty-four days later, when the Germans had been stopped and
thrown back to their starting line, more than twenty-nine American
divisions — 600,000 men — had joined the fight. Eighty-one thousand of
them were killed, wounded, or captured. Against us the Germans threw
more than twenty-eight divisions — half a million men. They lost a
hundred thousand of them."

The 9th Armored Division was placed along the whole Luxembourg
front, and this spread the armor of our division over the distance of
nearly a hundred miles. When the Germans attacked, every spearhead of
the German thrust immediately engaged the troops of the 9th Armored.
If nothing else, it must have been confusing for their intelligence people
to be reporting engaging armor of the 9th in every sector they entered.

Eight

The Ardennes: Battle of the Bulge

On January 4, 1945, Supreme Headquarters, Allied Expeditionary Forces (Public Relations Division), released this censored communiqué:

WITH THE 9TH ARMORED DIVISION: The 9th Armored Division, recently removed from the secret list, had a flaming introduction to battle. It crashed head-on into German armor in the current Von Rundstedt offensive and emerged with the admiration of even the enemy himself.

The Germans, finding combat teams of the 9th Armored fighting on such widely separated sectors of the front, gave the American division a name. German prisoners spoke of the 9th as the "Phantom Division." It was everywhere, they said, and they never could tell where its blows would be felt.

Utilizing its immense firepower to the utmost, even sending rear-echelon men into forward positions, the 9th Armored gave an admirable account of itself. In the vital sectors of the front — Bastogne, St. Vith, Echternach — there were 9th Armored combat teams fighting.

At one time in the battle, two bulges in the German lines stood out on the maps. They were at Echternach and St. Vith. In each of these bulges there were 9th Armored men, beating off violent German charges and even counterattacking. When the 9th's tanks were unable to get at the enemy armor, foot troops repulsed German tanks with bazookas.

The 9th is commanded by Major General John W. Leonard, who won the Distinguished Service Cross in the last war as the commander of an infantry battalion. He was wounded at Verdun and received the Purple Heart and two French decorations.

One combat team of the 9th fought a battle just east of Bastogne, which made the successful defense of that position possible. Tanks, artillery, and infantry of this combat command stood and slugged it out against all the assault power the Wehrmacht could offer. Meanwhile, American airborne forces and other armored units were gathering behind the 9th's combat command to defend the city itself.

After blunting the enemy spearhead and checking the headlong

German onrush westward, the 9th's combat command fell slowly back into Bastogne itself and continued to help defend the city. There were heroes of all ranks and positions in this combat team.

A second 9th Armored combat command, after a speedy march from the north, struck the Germans below St. Vith soon after they began their offensive. They smashed the Nazis back, only to find that its flanks were exposed. It then became necessary to fight a holding and delaying action.

The effect of this determined stand below St. Vith split the wedge the Germans had driven into Belgium and sapped the force of their efforts to wheel northward and capture vital Belgian cities.

Still a third combat command, operating on the southern flank, had a major part in confining the German steamroller to the northern areas of Luxembourg. This combat team defended the area around Echternach. The armored infantry battalion in this lineup frequently found itself fighting behind the German lines. It was a confused mêlée throughout.

In the battles of St. Vith, Bastogne, and Echternach, the 9th Armored Division wiped out large numbers of hardened German troops. It captured hundreds of prisoners and destroyed many German tanks.

When the German offensive began, the 9th Armored Division was the most powerful fighting unit present to oppose the initial onslaught.

Men of the 9th first faced the enemy in October in the hills of Luxembourg. General Leonard sent units of the division into the lines at that time so that they could become battle-conditioned, even though they were technically in reserve. The Germans definitely were not facing green troops.

The 9th Armored Division was activated at Camp Funston (Fort Riley), Kansas, July 15, 1942. After months of training there, it went through the California desert grind and participated in the Louisiana maneuvers. The 9th contains large numbers of former horse cavalrymen from the old 2nd Cavalry Division. There are other famous fighting units in the 9th. One, the 3rd Armored Field Artillery Battalion, dates its origin to 1794.

The 9th came overseas in August 1944. Vehicles were drawn in Southern England and the division crossed to France late in September.

Twice during the current offensive, the German radio reported the 9th Armored Division "destroyed." The Germans don't mention it anymore. They think they are seeing ghosts.

* * *

Another story, by the Orientation Branch, Information and Education Services, Headquarters, TSFET, is as follows:

SUPREME HEADQUARTERS
ALLIED EXPEDITIONARY
FORCE
(Public Relations Div)

Censored

For Immediate Release   January 4, 1945

With the 9th Armored Division: - The 9th Armored Division, recently removed from the secret list, had a flaming introduction to battle. It crashed
head-on into German armor in the current Rundstedt offensive and emerged with
the admiration of even the enemy himself.

The Germans, finding combat teams of the 9th Armored fighting on such
widely separated sectors of the front, gave the American division a name. German prisoners spoke of the 9th as the "Phantom Division". It was everywhere,
they said, and they never could tell where its blows would be felt.

Utilizing its immense firepower to the utmost, even sending rear echelon
men into forward positions, the 9th Armored gave an admirable account of itself.
In the vital sectors of the front, Bastogne, St. Vith, Echternach, there were
9th Armored combat teams fighting.

At one time in the battle two bulges in the German lines stood out on the
maps. They were at Echternach and St. Vith. In each one of these bulges there
were 9th Armored men, beating off violent German charges and even counterattacking. When the 9th's tanks were unable to get at the enemy armor, foot
troops repulsed German tanks with bazookas.

The 9th is commanded by Major General John W. Leonard, who won the Distinguished Service Cross in the last war as the commander of an infantry battalion. He was wounded at Verdun and received the Purple Heart and two French
decorations.

One combat team of the 9th fought a battle just east of Bastogne, that made
the successful defense of that position possible. Tanks, artillery and infantrymen of this combat command stood and slugged it out against all the assault
power the Wehrmacht could offer. Meanwhile American airborne forces and other
armored units were gathering behind the 9th's combat command to defend the city
itself.

After blunting the enemy spearhead and checking the headlong German onrush
westward, the 9th's combat command fell slowly back into Bastogne itself and
continued to help defend the city. There were heroes of all ranks and positions
in this combat team.

A second 9th Armored combat command, after a speedy march from the north,
struck the Germans below St. Vith soon after they began their offensive. They
smashed the Nazis back only to find that its flanks were exposed. It then
became necessary to fight a holding and delaying action.

The effect of this determined stand below St. Vith split the wedge the
Germans had driven into Belgium and sapped the force of their efforts to wheel
northward and capture vital Belgian cities.

- 1 -

January 4, 1945, press release.

Still a third combat command, operating on the southern flank, had a major part in confining the German steamroller to the northern areas of Luxembourg. This combat team defended the area around Echternach. The armored infantry battalion in this line-up frequently found itself fighting behind the German lines. It was a confused melee throughout.

In the battles of St. Vith, Bastogne and Echternach, the 9th Armored Division wiped out large numbers of hardened German troops. It captured hundreds of prisoners and destroyed many German tanks.

When the German offensive began, the 9th Armored Division was the most powerful fighting unit present to oppose the initial onslaught.

Men of the 9th first faced the enemy in October in the hills of Luxembourg. General Leonard sent units of the division into the lines at that time so they could become battle-conditioned, even though they were technically in reserve. The Germans definitely were not facing green troops.

The 9th Armored was activated at Camp Funston (Fort Riley), Kansas, July 15, 1942. After months of training there, it went through the California desert grind and participated in the Louisiana maneuvers. The 9th contains large numbers of former horse cavalrymen from the old 2nd Cavalry Division. There are other famous fighting units in the 9th. One, the 3rd Armored Field Artillery Battalion, dates its origin to 1794.

The 9th came overseas in August, 1944. Vehicles were drawn in Southern England and the division crossed to France late in September.

Twice during the current offensive the German radio reported the 9th Armored Division "destroyed". The Germans don't mention it any more. They think they are seeing ghosts.

* * * * * * *

(Reproduced Div Sig.O, Hq, 9th Armd Div, APO 259, U. S. Army, 5 February 1945.)

- 2 -

January 4, 1945, press release.

Troops of the 9th Armored Division felt somewhat like General Omar N. Bradley did about the Ardennes. They welcomed a German counterattack but they didn't want it to be so big. General Bradley since has spoken of the Remagen Bridge seizure and the Ardennes campaign as two of the turning points of the war. The fortunes of the 9th were strongly interwoven with both.

The Ardennes gave the 9th its first opportunity to show what it could do in a major battle. Its baptism was a bitter defensive action fought under the most difficult conditions. After the Ardennes, combat came much easier.

General Leonard sent his troops into the front lines for the first time along the Luxembourg-German frontier in October 1944, soon after they had arrived in the little duchy. Although the 9th Armored technically was in VIII Corps reserve, the division commander wanted the men to get the feel of combat. Because it was a relatively quiet sector, he obtained permission for the units to relieve other troops in the line for periods of conditioning.

The 9th underwent this battle training for nearly two months. Troops operated in a historic invasion area. The Eifel Hills had been selected by Von Rundstedt for his classic blitz in the spring of 1940. But this was 1944, it was winter, and the Americans were here now.

General Eisenhower and General Bradley paid the division a visit at Mersch, Luxembourg, in November. Infantry outfits were strung out along a wide sector of the front. The 9th was backing them up.

December 16, 1944: VIII Corps' sector came to life with a terrific roar. German artillery opened up all along the front. Infantry divisions in the line were the 106th, a new, untried outfit to the north, and the 28th and 4th, to the south, both of which had been exhausted by recent action.

Von Rundstedt hardly could have picked a more propitious time and place to strike the blow that stunned the allied world and carried the American forces close to disaster. He smashed his juggernaut into the weakest sector of the line and moved his panzer reserves behind the front with such cunning that the Nazi war machine was rolling at high speed before the Americans realized what was happening. Sheer guts saved the allies in the Ardennes. Ninth Armored men are quietly and deeply proud of their part in that heroic defense.

Widely spaced along the front, the 9th's three combat commands were forced to fight separately. CCB [Combat Command B] was at Faymonville, Belgium, twenty miles north of St. Vith, preparing to join the 2nd Infantry Division in capturing the Roer Dam, when enemy artillery rumbled over the ridges and buzz bombs roared over the town.

A platoon from the 811th Tank Destroyer Battalion took off immediately for St. Vith, key town in German plans and the center of a road network that Von Rundstedt wanted badly. When reports came in that the 106th Infantry Division was engaged in a fierce fight east of St. Vith, the entire command moved south.

Clattering through St. Vith at dawn, CCB received orders to attack and destroy enemy forces at Winterspelt. By this time, the Nazis had overrun the 106th's front and were driving up to St. Vith from the south. The 27th Armored Infantry Battalion struck this advancing German force with such power that it succeeded in pushing the Nazis back across the Our River.

Without flank protection, CCB was forced to pull back from the Our that night. This was the first of a series of disappointments for the command in the St. Vith action.

Next morning, a task force was sent north of the city to beat back an enemy armored column. One medium tank company of the 14th Battalion knocked out six tanks. CCB kept German forces out of St. Vith until relieved late on December 18.

German forces surged forth again in an effort to knock out the command's stronghold. In addition to the 1st SS Panzer and 62nd Volksgrenadier Divisions, Nazi units included elements of the 116th Panzer and the 18th Volksgrenadier Divisions.

Despite ammunition and food shortages, the lack of air support, and the constant threat of being cut off completely, CCB continued to smash the relentless attacks. An abandoned dump was located, rations salvaged by the men as they fought. Troops of the 9th Armored Engineer Battalion and the 89th Cavalry fought as infantrymen.

When the 27th Armored Infantry Battalion's CP [command post] was captured, General Hoge sent tanks and doughs [doughboys] to recapture it; they did. Although rumors spread among the troops that they were surrounded, men stuck to their guns. A BBC broadcast declared, "The brightest spot along the western front is at St. Vith."

"If this is a bright spot," remarked one GI, "what the hell is going on everywhere else?"

German artillery, which had been shelling CCB's CP ever since the beginning of the attacks, pounded dead on the target December 21. Six officers and men were killed, twenty were wounded.

Considerable heavy fighting continued before CCB withdrew from the sector and moved back over the escape route opened up by the 82nd Airborne Division. CCB had kept the enemy out of St. Vith for six days. The enemy paid a high price for his failure to take the town quickly.

CCA [Combat Command A], commanded by Brigadier General (then Colonel) Thomas L. Harrold, Troy, New York, defended a front-line sector near Beaufort, Luxembourg. The 60th Armored Infantry Battalion controlled the front when the Germans unpacked their power punch, and the entire combat command went into action when the magnitude of the attack was realized.

Four to five battalions of German artillery, ranging from 88s to 240s, pounded the sector. Telephone communications were knocked out immediately. Nazis then began infiltrating. A regiment of enemy infantry advancing southwest down Mullerthal Draw through the 4th Infantry Division sector attempted to get behind the 60th's positions. Artillery, mortars, and rockets pounded relentlessly.

Contact with the surrounded rifle companies was maintained only through a radio operated by Lieutenant Ira D. Cravens, Springfield, Illinois, forward observer for the 3rd Armored Field Artillery Battalion.

When CCA took over, it had instructions to maintain its positions until they became untenable. The command led off with a counterattack, December 18 — a counterattack that upset the 276th Volksgrenadier Division's schedule for the drive to Luxembourg City.

CCA now turned to aid its isolated rifle companies.

The Stars and Stripes gave this account of the withdrawal: "Nobody told the doughs of the 60th Armored Infantry Battalion to pull out, so they stayed and fought until word finally got through to them. A few days later they showed up in German helmets and with blankets draped over their shoulders, their rifles slung with bayonets fixed. They walked through German lines that way.... They kept right on going until they reached the U.S. lines. After that, they fought some more."

CCA held its sector in Luxembourg despite everything Germans threw at it. The 3rd Armored Field Artillery Battalion hurled thousands of shells into enemy positions, turned infantrymen when necessary. Tanks of the 19th Battalion broke up countless attacks while backing up the doughs. Recon men of the 89th Cavalry also fought as front-line riflemen.

When CCA was relieved December 26 by CCA of the 6th Armored Division, it experienced an even more severe test. Anticipating a rest, the combat command began a long night march to Etalle. While the column was on the road, orders were received that put CCA in the fight to relieve besieged Bastogne.

Without rest, and lacking time for sufficient preparation, General Harrold's troopers attacked the next morning. Hooking up with the 4th Armored Division, CCA carried on the fight until a corridor had been pounded through to Bastogne.

Still the fight continued. New Year's Eve, CCA thoroughly smashed a powerful German armor force that tried to cut Bastogne's supply corridor and isolate General Patton's spearheads. Thirty-two panzers were wrecked in a tremendous battle with 9th Armored's tanks.

The third combat command, CCR [Combat Command R], commanded by Colonel Joseph Gilbreth, Columbus, Georgia, perhaps had the roughest assignment of any outfit in the Ardennes. It was CCR that stood and slugged it out against the overwhelming might of the German panzers smashing toward Bastogne. Had it not been for CCR, Nazis would have taken the town before the 101st Airborne Division arrived there to make its historic stand.

Small CCR task forces of tanks from the 2nd Tank Battalion and doughs of the 52nd Armored Infantry Battalion took up positions along the roads leading to Bastogne from the east. Their mission was to block the roads at all cost. They clung to their positions even when surrounded. Masses of German tanks rolled around them; enemy infantry infiltrated in the darkness.

There were no front lines in this melée. Artillerymen, tankers, and engineers fought as doughs. The 2nd Tank Battalion encountered elements of nine German divisions. The 73rd Armored Field Artillery Battalion fought its way out of a trap, kept its guns in action.

Although casualties were heavy and all three of its battalion commanders lost, CCR was officially credited with delaying the enemy for thirty-six to forty-eight hours east of Bastogne. When its surviving forces fell back into Bastogne, CCR was assigned to maintain a mobile reserve known as Task Force Snafu (a makeshift mobile fighting force that could move rapidly wherever needed).

TF Snafu became a potent force in the ensuing battles. Organized chiefly as a troubleshooter for the 101st, this unit operated on a ten-minute alert and sped to threatened areas as needed. Bolstered by armor, it proved to be an ace in the hole.

CCR received the Presidential Unit Citation for its action at Bastogne.

Because its forces were widely separated, 9th Armored's outstanding fight in the Ardennes didn't receive the attention it deserved until the battle was over. Then, military men pointed out the remarkable job the division had accomplished. Commendations came from two army commanders, General Courtney H. Hodges and General George S. Patton, Jr., from three army corps and four divisions.

By training and background, 9th Armored troops were well equipped for the furious Ardennes fighting and for succeeding roles.

Made up largely of former horse cavalrymen of the famous 2nd

Cavalry Division, the 9th was activated July 15, 1942, at Fort Riley (Camp Funston), Kansas. One unit, the 3rd Armored Field Artillery Battalion, dates its battle record back to 1794. It fought in every major military campaign in American history.

The 9th trained for nearly a year at the Fort Riley reservation, then went to the Mojave Desert near Needles, California, for additional hardening. Reorganized as a light armored division, the 9th participated in Louisiana maneuvers, where its army commander was General Hodges.

* * *

The above two documented stories pretty well set the stage of the situation in Luxembourg at that time. A messenger was sent from our unit to Bastogne, but not long after leaving the company area, he ran into an enemy ambush. This is one of those incredible stories that comes from the war. A German machine gun fired at the rate of 1,200 bullets a minute, ours only fired at 400. In essence, a German machine gun fired three times to every shot that ours would fire. When the messenger was caught in the ambush, the German gunner opened up on him and he had to back up and turn around. He couldn't make a U-turn because the road was too narrow. All the time, he was under the deadly fire of that gun. He and his passenger returned to the company area with the windshield of the Jeep shattered and the steering wheel smashed. He found eleven bullets in his duffel bag. Neither he nor his passenger was hit. It was impossible to figure out where they were when the bullets went through.

One of our fellows received an excruciatingly painful shrapnel wound to the hand. His buddy took him to the aid station and decided to stay with him to try to comfort him. An 88 hit the aid station, and the wounded man was killed. His buddy, the good samaritan, was severely wounded in the stomach and was evacuated to a hospital in England. Because of the extent of his injuries, he was supposed to be sent to a hospital in the United States. But there was another fellow in the hospital with the same last name, and a mixup occurred. The other fellow was sent home instead. By the time the officials discovered the mistake, the doctor had declared our guy fit for active duty and he was returned to our outfit — just in time to be captured.

There was mass confusion about what was going on, but we pulled out of Schoenfels immediately. The fourteen-year-old son of the Strauss family begged to go with us, and we almost had to use force to leave him behind. We moved into an area where the 119th Regiment of the 28th Infantry Division was digging foxholes and slit trenches behind us. I walked over to them and said that they had this thing all wrong — they should be up in front of us. There was no smile or response, so I decided to leave well enough alone.

We were providing radio communications for G-2 (intelligence) of the division. Word spread throughout the front that the Germans had massacred captives and were not taking prisoners. This suddenly became the unspoken policy, but it created a problem for intelligence. They had to have prisoners to provide information about the enemy. Direct orders were given that prisoners would in fact be taken. It is amazing how word can travel through a battle area, but everyone on the front seemed to know immediately about the German massacre of our troops at Malmedy.

Those nights were the blackest nights that I can ever remember. Standing guard in the dark, I would wave my hand in front of my eyes in an attempt to see something — but I could see absolutely nothing. To make matters worse, something was falling from the trees and making noises out in the dark, and we would listen for the sound of a weapon firing. It was easy to identify the slow, dull thud of an American machine gun in comparison to the sharp, rapid fire of the German burp gun or machine gun.

The engineers were placing huge blocks of TNT on the sides of the trees along the roads. This was in preparation for our withdrawal, so that they could drop those trees across the road after our units had pulled back. All guns were firing, but unfortunately, with the capture of the 106th Infantry, all codes and transmissions were neutralized. The heavy firing had cut most of the telephone lines, but half of those would be broken by the tanks also. Radio was still operating, but you couldn't trust what you were receiving. We received direct orders to move two miles behind what we knew to be enemy lines. This message was received in code and had been authenticated. We were now reduced to not having any reliable manner of transmitting or receiving messages. To explain this, we would transmit messages in five letter groups, and the receiving station would take those five letter groups and feed them into a code machine. The code machine would be set to a specific secret setting, and a clear text message would come out. The Germans had all our codes — even the code names of our units, including our code machines. For instance, our company was code-named David and our division was code-named Combat. When a message was sent, they immediately knew who sent it and to whom. Messengers were unable to get through, our telephone lines were either cut or tapped, and all our codes were in enemy hands. When we would make a telephone call (if the line had not been cut), the Germans would answer, using the code name of the unit we were calling. We were in desperate straits. Before we realized that the Germans had all of our codes, we played right into their hands by transmitting messages that they could decode. It was tremendously frustrating not to know which messages were real and which were substitutes sent by the Germans. Each message was acted upon depending on whether or not it was considered authentic. It was a hell of a way to fight a war. The units that came in behind us had the luxury — if you can call it that — of knowing that their messages were secure. We were not able to get our communication systems back on track until after the Battle of the Bulge.

Members of the division band would usually kid us about their job with the division. They would say things like, "While you fellows are out there sweating your butts off, we will be playing gentle little tunes so that the general can sleep peacefully." When our units began to withdraw through the Ardennes, the military police usually would direct traffic. The usual question from an MP was, "How do I know when the last American vehicle has passed?" The answer was, "When you see the first German." This basically was true, and we lost a number of MPs as a result. The division band was sent in to supplement the MPs, and unfortunately we lost a number of them, also.

In school I had read about the conscription of men during the Revolutionary War, but the Battle of the Bulge had its conscription also. The American people are curious and generally want to see what is going on. This was true during the Bulge as well, and rear-echelon troops would hitch a ride with messengers or, using one excuse or another, get the use of a vehicle to come look around. The units were desperate for replacements, and these tourists would be ordered out of the vehicles — all except the driver — and conscripted to fill the empty slots. These men had been curious about what was happening, and now they would get the information firsthand. Some of them took their new duties seriously, but others took the first opportunity to return to their home bases.

During this period, we heard shells going over our heads from the rear. These were really big ones, and it sounded like ashcans were flying over and exploding ahead. At first we thought we had been surrounded, but then we found out that these were our 240s and 155s firing in support of our units.

A fellow arrived and asked me for a cleaning rod for his gun, so I laughed and said, "Buddy, shoot it clean!" He said, "I can't — it has cosmoline in it and I have to get it out." (Cosmoline is a thick grease that they use to preserve new guns.) I was shocked, so I said, "Where in hell have you come from?" He answered, "I just arrived from Paris, where I had been flown in from North Carolina, and rushed up here." I didn't know what was happening anywhere else on the front, but this certainly didn't sound like a Happy New Year. I advised him to throw away the gun and pick up another one, but he told me he was charged out with it. My response to that is better left unprinted. I never found out what he did or where he went. The most frightening aspect of this incident was that someone in the rear was panicking and ordering men to the front without checking to see that all of their gear and weapons were combat-ready. How bad was the situation around us? We had no way of knowing.

Here's another story that made the rounds — one I believe is true. General Patton arrived up at the CCA command post and strutted in with his pearl-handled pistols. Colonel Harrold looked up at him and stated, "You I don't need, ammunition I do!" General Patton left, and supplies and reinforcements followed.

We had all been told that the quartermaster at the railhead at Arlon, Belgium, was arranging Christmas dinner for all the troops in the area. But the Stukas, as a first mission, dive-bombed the railhead, and all of those turkeys took their last flight. Christmas dinner had been totally destroyed. That, I suppose, was the least of our worries.

On December 24, we were ordered to regroup at Fratin, Belgium, and most of us were able to make it during the day. Our crew was taken in by the Colignon family, who lived on a small farm at the edge of town. The family members were wonderful to us, and they heated bath water on the big kitchen stove. They had a regular wash tub, and I was sitting in the tub in the living room when two women came in to test the water. I can still recall sitting in the water, my knees up around my ears, listening to those two women discussing, in French, the temperature of the water. At least that's what I think they were discussing. As soon as they left, I was out of that tub and dressed in no time.

There was an attractive young daughter, Nelly Colignon, whom we adopted during the time we were there. We knew that some of the men would try to make a pass at her, and we were just as determined that we would protect her. She was a nice girl.

Mr. Colignon called aside one of the men and took him to the barn. There he had secreted a hand gun that was well oiled and in working condition. During the five years of the German occupation of his country, he had kept that gun, despite knowing that if he were caught, he would be executed. These people appreciated their freedom, and they were thankful that we were there.

The C-47 cargo planes came right across the rooftops of town in their

Nelly Colignon and her father, Fratin, Belgium. (Right) The Colignon family, Fratin, Belgium. This family was good to us.

run to resupply the trapped troops at Bastogne. As soon as they went over us, they zoomed upward in order to get enough height to drop their supplies. When they did this, they came under murderous antiaircraft fire from the Germans. I saw fourteen C-47s tumbling from the sky, and the air was full of parachutes. Those with Jeeps were told to chase down the parachutes and either rescue or capture the chutist. We didn't know ahead of time whether they were friend or enemy, but most of them were ours. It was humorous to hear them talking about chasing a parachute. A Jeep had to stick to the roads, but the chute would just follow the wind. The Jeep had to race pell-mell to try to stay with the chutist.

The parish priest of the church in Fratin went to the commanding officer and told him that ever since the allies had freed the town a few months earlier, he and the parishioners had been planning a beautiful midnight Christmas service. He asked permission to go forward with the service. The CO flatly refused, saying that the enemy was within firing distance and any light could be disastrous. Evidently the priest was very convincing, pleading that since the people hadn't had a Christmas service in more than five years, they would do anything to have it this year. The CO finally approved, with the admonition that the guards would fire at any light that showed. Word spread around town that there would be a midnight service, and Catholic, Jew, and Protestant alike decided it might not be a bad idea to attend. We needed all the help we could get.

Imagine going to a Christmas Eve service armed to the teeth — which is just what we did, about twenty or thirty of us. Entering the church was like entering another world. The warmth, sanctity, safety, and familiarity of the surroundings were tremendously reassuring. Most of us sat in the rear of the church, but pews were never designed for a fully armed soldier. There was no place to stash a rifle, and we put our helmets on the wooden floor. Every now and then, a rifle would slip and crash to the floor, or someone would accidentally kick a helmet and it would roll along the floor. Despite all this racket, the people did not seem to mind, and we appreciated being there, even though we were embarrassed by the disruption we caused. We noticed that the choirboys were giggling and acting up. I thought it strange, but then I was in a strange country. The service was in French, but we got the general gist of it, and it was beautiful and memorable. This was my third Christmas in the service, and the most meaningful of all.

As we left the church after the service, under a full moon, a German Junkers 88 flew right over us with one engine on fire. I could clearly see the two pilots in the blister in front desperately trying to control the aircraft. That plane, with its right engine blazing, passed in front of the moon, and, oddly enough, it was a colorful and memorable sight. We never did hear the plane crash.

The following morning, we found out what had made the choirboys giggle. Most of our company had come into town during the day, but some had arrived after dark. The ones who arrived after dark were advised by the outpost guards to find a barn or shelter and bed down for the night. Naturally, at that hour, all the houses were closed. One of them tried the church and found the door open. So six of them entered the church, threw their bedrolls down around the altar, and went to sleep. When the priest arrived for the mass, he saw the men and realized they were exhausted, so he decided not to disturb them. The choirboys were giggling at these men in bedrolls lying around the altar.

The part of this story that really broke us up was that the men were asleep when the service started. Hearing them explain their reactions was worth the price of admission. One fellow heard the church music and immediately thought, "I've bought it. This must be heaven." Then, when he lowered the zipper on his bedroll and saw the kids giggling, all he wanted to do was get out of there. The consensus was that it was the longest service they had ever slept through.

The 60th Armored Infantry Battalion was alliterative and brief in its summary of action during the German counteroffensive. The battalion's account: "Battered bastards battled from Beaufort and Bigelback to bastion of Bastogne on Belgian border in Battle of the Bulge."

During the Battle of the Bulge, spies infiltrated into our units. The most famous of these was a German dressed in a U.S. Army captain's uniform who drove a captured Jeep into Bastogne. He toured the city, observing the defenses, and then drove out. Not until he had left did they begin to question who he was. In most cases, because of the confusion, we accepted anyone in a U.S. uniform as one of ours. Thus, it was not difficult for spies to operate, although what was confusing to us had to be just as confusing to them. I had no personal knowledge of a spy operating in our area, but then if you don't catch them, you never know.

One dark night, I was challenged, and I responded, "I'm an American." A disgusted voice responded, "So am I, I'm a Canadian!"

A statistician figured out that every gun in our division fired every eleven seconds for eleven days. Whether or not that was accurate or close to accurate, the fact was that our guns were worn out and there was no rifling left in them. Our gunners were firing and the shells would leave the guns and bounce along the ground until they hit a contact point. It was time to get the division out of there. We were given orders to withdraw to Sedan, France, in order to draw new equipment and replacements. We had suffered forty-four percent casualties in that melée.

One factor I have never understood about this whole affair was how it could have happened. Here we were facing a daunting enemy and we were never advised of a huge and massive buildup of men and equipment. We had superior air power and observation facilities. I have always felt that the euphoria of the tremendously successful invasion of the continent on D day, and the sweep across France, had given allied leaders a sense of invincibility. They must have ignored signs that would have been recognized immediately under normal conditions. I am no military expert, but I have always felt that there was a huge error in judgment that almost led to a major defeat. What happened probably shortened the war in the long run because of the huge losses in men, supplies, and equipment sustained by the enemy. Also, the casualty figures in this battle, though high, probably were less than in a drawn-out struggle. Although the divisions along the line paid the price for an apparent miscalculation, the enemy paid a heavier price in men and equipment by not being able to attain their objective. In all probability, the biggest mistake in the Battle of the Bulge was made by German intelligence. Axis Sally knew where our division was located, but German intelligence had placed it with the 9th Army, 100 miles north of where we actually were. Therefore, they grossly underestimated the firepower of the American forces facing them in the Ardennes.

We were awarded our second battle star, the Ardennes, to be placed on our European, African, Middle Eastern Theater Campaign Ribbon.

There is no accurate count of enemy casualties inflicted by our division because we were not fighting as a division, but there is no question that they were heavy. We paid the price for being there, and they paid the price because we were.

An interesting point of all this is that we sailed across the ocean in probably the largest single transport of troops that has ever taken place, and the ship was called the "Gray Ghost." Then we were thinly stationed all along the Luxembourg-Belgian area — the "ghost front." And, finally, the Germans, in the largest battle the United States has ever fought, called us the "Phantom Division."

Left to right: McAvoy, Bob Fulton, Byrne Waterman, and Larry Reichard. This was a reunion at Poix-Terron, France.

Dismantled Maginot Line pillbox, Poix-Terron, Sedan, France.

Nine

Sedan and Metz, France; Liège, Belgium; Roer Valley, Germany

The 9th Armored Division gradually withdrew from the Battle of the Bulge and reassembled in Sedan, France, where it was bitterly cold. Replacements and new equipment were forthcoming until the division was back to full strength. We moved into that area at night with blackout lights, and I remarked at the time that if we were ever captured, they would be able to report that the GIs were poorly dressed and inadequately equipped. My feet, standing on the metal floor of the half-track, were almost frozen. I took a blanket, cut it into strips, and wound the strips around my feet. Instead of wearing my combat boots, I wore my overshoes to keep my feet warm. It was far from pleasant.

Our company was now back together again, and we spent time swapping lies and getting together with old friends. The area we were in was dotted with the fortifications of the old French Maginot Line. This line had been supposed to be impregnable, but the French had built it so that the guns could fire only toward Germany. Once the Germans breached that line, all the rest of the fortifications were attacked from the rear, and they fell like dominoes. In our spare time, we toured these dismantled fortifications.

About this time, all of us were sent to a portable shower unit — and what a pleasure that was! We would walk in and place our rifle, helmet, personal possessions (wallet and watch), and boots in a basket and then strip off all the rest of our clothes. Then we would be given a large bath towel and soap and enter the hot shower. After showering, we would receive clean underwear, uniform, etc., and then pick up our personal items and leave. It was fantastic to be clean from the skin out. We had lived in those unwashed clothes for a long time.

We had been issued impregnated clothing to go along with our gas masks in case of a chemical-warfare attack. Included in that gear was a wool hood that covered my head and shoulders and formed an opening around my eyes to just below my lips. I had a knitted wool scarf that my mother had given me, and I wound that around my head so it covered my nose and mouth from just below my eyes. Between the hood and that

Fort near Metz with blown bridges.

scarf, I was able to keep from getting frostbite, although there were ice balls in front of my mouth when I breathed.

One night I decided to sleep in a bombed-out house instead of outside on the open ground. At the time, it seemed like a good idea. Naturally, with part of the walls blown out and the winds whistling through that house, I was frozen — even in my bedroll. In the middle of the night, I moved out of the house and threw my bedroll on the snow, where I slept — nice and warm — for the rest of the night. After that, I was pretty selective about where I chose to sleep. Sometimes you learn fast.

It was somewhere around this time that we drew the new General Pershing tank, a forty-ton beast that was the equal of the German Tiger tank. For the first time, our tanks were on an equal footing with the power of the Tiger tank. The Tiger's gun was an 88mm, and the Pershing had a 90mm gun. Although I cannot confirm this, I believe that the Pershing was a copy of the Tiger tank that was taken back to Detroit and redesigned. When the Pershings first saw action, the Germans would see the silhouette of the tank and not fire at it. Too late, they would realize their mistake. Up until that time, our most powerful tank had been the General Sherman, a thirty-ton tank with a 76mm gun.

Metz Cathedral, Metz, France. The photo was taken from far away, as the cathedral is huge. Many windows were shattered.

We soon learned that the local people considered C-rations a delicacy, and we could trade a can of C-rations for a bucket of wine (about two and a half to three quarts). Almost every house had a wine cellar, so this helped to spark up our meals. We also used bouillon powder on the C-ration to change the flavor of it. It did help.

The army found that the troops were hesitant to use needles when someone was wounded and needed an injection. (We all carried a small medic kit that contained morphine.) So when our inoculations came due, we were told that instead of a medic giving us the shots, we would have to buddy up and give them to each other. This wasn't my cup of tea, but I did pretty well. Then it was my buddy's turn. He gave me as good a shot as I had ever received from a medic, and I told him so. His response was, "It's no wonder, I do the pigs at home all the time."

In order to provide some camouflage, all of our vehicles had been whitewashed. They had a mottled white appearance that blended in perfectly with the winter background of snow. When the division was pretty much back to full strength, we were given orders to move to the area near Metz, along the Moselle River in France. We were to line up along the Moselle because the Germans were there, but they were quiet

Argancy, France: Our whitewashed vehicle and the house where we stayed in the rear of the church.

and our commanders did not expect any action from them. Where had we heard that before?

We had received a replacement in our unit and the fellow seemed rather moody, but everyone usually tended to his own business. This went on for some time, and then one day he burst out, "I have to know. What happened to the guy I am replacing?" Evidently, it had really been bothering him.

We traveled beyond Metz and moved into a town called Argancy, which was almost totally deserted. We parked our vehicle in a narrow street behind the church and occupied a home that was across from the rear of the church. We were to spend the rest of January and February in that area. As in Luxembourg, it was very quiet along that line.

Sometime in February, we were surprised to receive a full Christmas dinner with all the fixings. We looked at each other and remarked that it renewed our faith in Santa Claus.

One day while we were standing idly by our vehicles, some members of the FFI (Free French of the Interior), in uniform, came peddling up to the church on bicycles. They laid down their bikes gently, drew their pistols from their holsters, and surrounded the church. We were most interested in what was going on. Here we were with all the firepower that they might need, yet they were doing this on their own with their

Argancy, France, church where three spies were operating.

little hand guns. When they were ready, they moved stealthily into the church, and it wasn't long before out they came with three prisoners. It seems these traitors had been operating a radio from the steeple of the church, and when they needed anything, they stole it from our vehicles. The FFI — proud as punch — left town with their prisoners in tow. We were actually dumbfounded.

Since things were pretty quiet, some of the fellows would roam around, and one of them located a brewery in the next town, right along the river. He told us that there were bottles — huge bottles — of booze in the brewery, and it was there for the taking. On some excuse or other, we acquired a truck and headed to the town. We parked the truck by the brewery and had started to load the booze into it when one of the fellows signaled to us. He was at the rear of the building, looking out the window at the river. There, on the other side, was a German officer out for a stroll — slowly walking along with his hands clasped behind his back. Our guy raised his rifle, remarking that he would pick off that SOB. But we grabbed him and pulled him from the window. We had no idea why this town wasn't occupied by either side, but it didn't seem like a good idea for us to start anything when we would have to explain what we were doing there in the first place and how we acquired the truck in the second place. We loaded the truck with booze and took it back to

Camouflaged pillbox, part of the Maginot Line. The location is unknown, as this was a German photo.

Argancy. It was here that we started our practice of filling one of our vehicle's five-gallon water cans with booze.

There were two five-gallon cans mounted — one on each side of the vehicle just forward of the front seat on the outside. All through the rest of the war, the main argument was whether or not we really needed both five-gallon cans of water. There were times when we would acquire some pretty good brew, and it was a shame to pass it up, but we were already well stocked. Somehow common sense prevailed, and one five-gallon can had the best brew that we could acquire and the other carried that much-debated five gallons of water.

Mess was served about a block away from the house where we were staying, and we would take our mess kits and walk to it. Halfway to the mess lived an old French man with his dog, and when I walked by the first day, the dog bellowed away at me. The second day, he came running toward me. I have always enjoyed dogs and have gotten along well with them, but this dog kept coming at me. For some reason, he bit me on the knee. The third day, when I walked past, the dog charged again, but this time I was ready for him and caught him in the chin with my boot. After that, he would stand on the stoop every day and bark at me, but he never made another move.

It was in Argancy that I made some ice cream from a mess cup of snow, a teaspoon of cocoa, a little sugar, and some evaporated milk. It didn't taste bad at that time, but I would hate to try it today.

After about two months in Argancy, we received orders to move to Liège, Belgium. The whole division once again was on the move, and since this meant moving about 3,000 vehicles, it was a major project. We arrived in Liège and were billeted in a mansion just outside of town. When I went to the latrine, I found that it had two stools in it — this was the first time I had ever seen a bidet. It quickly became the topic of conversation, and in fact it was almost a tourist attraction, because everyone wanted to see it and see how it worked.

Soon we were ordered to start moving out against the Germans in the Roer Valley. Suddenly we found that a new shavetail, a second lieutenant, was to be assigned to our crew. We were pretty disgruntled about it, because these guys usually move in with all their barracks training of spit and polish and want to do everything by the book. We had our own ideas of how we wanted to do things. The lieutenant greeted us and took his position in the vehicle. After we were riding along for a while, he turned and said, "I don't know where you guys have stowed it, but I sure would like a drink." We laughed and handed him a canteen, which was full of booze. We weren't alcoholics, but I am inclined to think that we could have taught some of them a few tricks.

When not expecting enemy action, we would keep the machine gun unloaded, but when moving up, we would put it in the half-load position. This meant that before we could fire it, we would have to pull the bolt back and release it, and that would fully load the gun. There were two ways of loading the machine gun. One was to open the top, lay the belt of bullets through the gun, jack the bolt, and then close the cover. The other way was to feed the belt of bullets into the gun and jack the bolt one time to half load. The difference here was that when we loaded it with the cover open, the gun was fully loaded, not half loaded. As we started to move up, the machine gun — which was on a post in the middle of our vehicle — swung around with the motion of the vehicle until it was pointing at me. I pushed it away, but the motion of the vehicle brought it back in line with me again. Again I pushed it away, and then I noticed that the gun was getting a little help: One of the fellows was giving it a nudge to make it line up with me. I had always been taught that you don't point a gun at anyone unless you intend to shoot him, so I expressed my opinion in no uncertain terms. The fellow laughed, said, "Hell, it's not loaded," pointed the gun skyward, and squeezed the trigger. He expected to hear a click, but instead a short burst came from the gun. One of the bullets was a tracer that seemed to hang in the sky forever. We caught hell for firing that burst, and from then on, we all took a lot more care in handling that gun.

We had been briefed that we were now entering hostile territory, and we needed to be prepared for it. In the other countries, we had been conquering heroes, but in Germany we would be strictly the enemy. But they had forgotten one major point: In order to keep the factories and support industries operating, the Germans had displaced ten million people. As we entered Germany, these people — from India, the Arab countries, the Baltics, etc. — were there to greet us. It was a shock, and totally unexpected, to see people waving greetings to us, even people in Arab dress.

We pulled into one town for the night and ordered a family to move across the street while we occupied their home. The man had two young daughters of about eighteen and nineteen years of age, and we were moving in while they were moving out. Every time the girls would enter the bedroom to pick up some things, the father stood in the doorway with his hand in his pocket. The thought went through my head that he had a gun in there, but then I shrugged it off, thinking that he wouldn't be that stupid. This happened two or three times, and I almost accosted him, except that his daughters had finished collecting everything they needed and were leaving. The man stepped up to the lieutenant and handed him the gun he had had in his pocket. Apparently, if any of our guys had accosted his daughters, he would have opened fire. I made up my mind right there that I wouldn't take anything for granted from then on.

We arrived at a factory at the end of a long day, tired and hungry, and were dropping our bedrolls and looking for space to sleep when we received emergency orders to pull out. We were throwing our bedrolls in the half-track as it was rolling out of the factory yard, and of course we were bitching in good shape. We weren't a mile from the factory when the Stukas dive-bombed it, and I thought to myself that I owed some spy — or someone who had intercepted a message — a very large thank you. Needless to say, the bitching stopped immediately. That factory was reduced to rubble in moments — those planes had a mission to destroy the factory, and that mission was carried out. We quietly consumed our cold rations that night.

One morning in early March, it was cold, wet, raining, and miserable when I went to the mess for breakfast. I was surprised to be issued five bottles of Coca-Cola, and I was told to return the empties at dinner that evening. When I asked what had brought this about, I was told that the Coca-Cola plant in Liège had just been reactivated, but they had to have the bottles back that evening. It was too miserable a day even to think about consuming a cold soda. I drank two of the Cokes and returned three unopened bottles with the empties. We were never issued any Cokes after that, but then we were steadily moving away from that plant.

Something came up for which a messenger had to be sent immediately, and the CO ordered me to take a Jeep and do the job. I told him I did not have a driver's license, but he immediately turned to the first sergeant and ordered him to give me a license. Nobody asked me whether or not I could drive. The sergeant immediately wrote out a license and pointed out the Jeep I should take. I had never had driving instructions but had been a passenger when others were learning how to drive. I took the Jeep and it started to leapfrog out of the motor pool. When I reached a corner, an MP was directing traffic and stopped all traffic to let me through. He made a sweeping bow as I leapfrogged past him, laughing all the time. The upshot of this is that I drove quite a few Jeeps, half-tracks, and 6X6 trucks while in Germany, and when I returned to the States, I exchanged my army driver's license for a Maine license. To this date, I have never taken a driver's test, although I have taken the safe driving course.

Our crew consisted of six men in a half-track. Here's a list of the duties of each one: The driver had the responsibility for the operation of the vehicle, especially to keep the battery charged because of the drain we placed on it with the radio, sending and receiving. The crew chief was a radio operator, staff sergeant, whose responsibility was the whole crew but also the scheduling of all of us on a twenty-four-hour-a-day communication system. Three of us were radio operators, and the last was the codeman or message-center man, who was responsible for the codes and code machine. (All of us also knew how to operate the code machine.) When the vehicle was stationary, naturally all of us were not expected to stay close to it, so sometimes we were available for other tasks. We also had some time to roam around like tourists. As long as the radio was covered by someone, we were free to find something else to do. Many times, we almost felt like observers of the war.

We had a French man — whom we named "Frenchie" — with us from the FFI. He was a likable cuss, and one day we picked up some booze that was like white lightning. I took a swig of it and then had to grab my chest to hang on while it burned its way down. It must have been 150 proof (proof being fifty percent pure alcohol). When I finally was able to catch my breath, I saw Frenchie and called him over, telling him I had some great booze. I poured four to six ounces of the stuff into my mess cup and gave it to him. He took it and drank it right down, smacking his lips and saying, "C'est bon!" I couldn't believe it — he must have had a cast-iron stomach.

One day, I noticed a few men working through the wreckage of a B-17 that had crashed months earlier. When I asked them what they were doing, they said they were with the Graves Identification Unit and were trying to identify members of the crew of that aircraft. Not having anything to do at that moment, I worked along with them, looking for identification bracelets, dog tags, wristwatches with serial numbers on them, anything that would identify the men. They were very thorough. It was a thankless job, as that aircraft had hit the ground with tremendous force and pieces were spread out over a number of acres. And, having been down that long, the plane had been pretty well looted by the local residents.

We were pressing ahead toward the Rhine River when the rear wheels of a twenty-ton engineering truck broke through the pavement at a crossroads and the axle became hung up on the pavement. It was pouring rain, and the area was the usual quagmire that a tank division can make of mud. When we approached, an MP was desperately trying to do something. An 88 was firing, and we knew that it was only a matter of time before he zeroed in on us. We attached our winch to the rear axle of the truck and began to wind it in, but the weight of the truck made us skid into it. Every time an 88 would whistle in, the MP would hit the dirt (mud), so he was the saddest sight I had seen for a long time. The driver of the engineering truck unwound the winch from his vehicle and encircled a brick house that was nearby. As he pulled up on his winch, bricks began falling off the wall. At the same time, we were beginning to skid into the rear of the truck. All of a sudden, at the last moment, the combined efforts of all of us produced enough power to pull him out. We were thankful to leave that spot.

As we moved closer to the Rhine, suddenly we were joined by the U.S. Navy with pontoon boats and pontoons. We kidded them that they had missed a turn and that the ocean was 300 miles the other way. Those units turned into a godsend, but at the time, it seemed ridiculous that they should be so far forward. We got a big kick out of one of the navy men, who said he had joined the navy because he didn't want anything to do with the army, mud, etc.

We moved into this town in the rain, as usual, and the major asked a couple of us to accompany him into a home. The hostility of the people was evident, and we moved through the rooms until we came to what looked like a dining room with the doors closed. We ordered them to open the doors. Inside was a man laid out, covered by a sheet up to his neck, with a candle burning near his head. He had been killed the day before in the air strike. Incongruously, I thought, "Migosh, he's dead." Seeing someone laid out seemed to make a great difference and bring the whole ordeal closer to home. I never did know what the major was

*Irving Bransky with
the machine gun.
Bazooka shells are in
cylinders on the floor.*

looking for, but we could have cut the hate in that house with a knife.

As we left the house, a sergeant I didn't know stopped the major and advised him that they had just caught a spy. The major asked him if he was sure. The sergeant responded that they had him dead to rights. The major then said, "Take care of him!" That was the shortest trial I have ever witnessed. A few weeks later, I would reflect seriously on that conversation.

I don't know whether it always rained during the war, but my memories are mostly of sloppy, muddy messes. Now and then, however, there would be a beautiful day. There couldn't have been many of them, but there were some. I do know that a tank division creates a mud that is the creamiest and sloppiest of all muds. I suppose, too, that the constant hammering of the bombs and shells would cause more rain than usual.

We were awarded our third battle star, Central Europe, to be attached to the European, African, Middle Eastern Theater Campaign Medal.

One day, I was on the radio when I received a clear text message (this was extremely unusual, as all messages were coded) that stated, "We have taken the Remagen railroad bridge across the Rhine." That message brought about a whole realignment of the thinking and objectives of our units. All units were ordered immediately to move to the bridge, bumper to bumper, flaunting regulations that require a spacing of a hundred yards between vehicles to reduce casualties. This was to be an all-out effort to save the bridge and secure the bridgehead. On the other side of the Rhine, the Germans were ordered to destroy the bridge at all costs. The Germans had made a mistake, and now it was our turn to capitalize on it.

Rhine Bridge Nazi Gift To Ninth Armd.

By Andy Rooney
Stars and Stripes Staff Writer

EAST OF THE RHINE, Mar. 9— The strangest fighting force which ever established a bridgehead moved across the Rhine at Remagen Wednesday on a quarter-mile long railway bridge.

A Ninth Armored Div. combat command under Brig. Gen. William Hoge reached the Rhine at Remagen at about 1530 and ran into the greatest surprise the Germans have sprung on the First Army since D-Day. The Ludendorff bridge was intact. Hoge, a former engineer himself, immediately scrapped all other plans and called Maj. Gen. John W. Leonard at Ninth Armored headquarters. The decision was made immediately to push men across and exploit the greatest piece of luck the American Army has had during this war.

The platoon from 2/Lt. Carl Timmerman's Able company, commanded by 2/Lt. Emmett Burrows, moved across first and was followed by three more companies from Maj. Murray Devers' 27th Armored Infantry Battalion.

Before dark Gen. Hoge had pushed across every man and vehicle he could take from the area and by noon the following day the roads on the east side of the Rhine leading from the bridge area were crowded.

Brilliant Tactical Maneuver

The quick change of plans and immediate utilization of available fighting forces was a brilliant tactical maneuver. Security, which yesterday was supposed to leave everyone guessing as to whether Americans swam, rowed or bridged the Rhine, was lifted to some extent today but the size and composition of the bridgehead force is still on the secret list.

The bridge stretches across the Rhine between the two small German towns of Erpel and Remagen just north along the river from Coblenz. It is a three-span, steel truss railroad bridge which arches magnificently across the Rhine. The east side of the bridge runs directly into a sharp rising hill and the railroad tracks disappear into a tunnel. The sharp rise behind the east approach to the bridge makes it difficult for German artillery to shell the structure.

As Burrows' platoon approached the bridge to make the first crossing, the doughs more than half expected that it would be blown to bits under their feet. As they came up the approach a German soldier, on their side of the bridge touched off pre-set demolition charges and raced for the east side hoping to escape. The demolitions went off and slight damage was done to the bridge. The soldier who actually set off the charges somehow escaped but several other Germans were killed in the middle of the span 75 feet above the racing Rhine.

Engineers Work Under Fire

The bridge was under small arms and 20mm fire up to 2200 Wednesday. Engineers from "B" Company of the Ninth Armored Engineers went to work on the necessary minor repairs under the direction of 1/Lt. John Mitchell, of Pittsburgh. They worked all night and completed their task after three of them had been killed by small arms snipers.

The engineers' first job when they hit the bridge was to start cutting wires. They all grabbed wire cutters and started cutting every wire on the bridge or within a quarter mile of it.

The anti-aircraft outfits, some of which had never fired at German planes before, scored a perfect four for four yesterday and today, when at 0900 three more German bombers came over, they scored with two out of three. One German bomb nicked the bridge but it was undamaged.

While the Germans threw about 30 shells an hour into Remagen and sent their planes over the tankers, doughs on the east bank of the Rhine mostly sat around and waited for the reshuffling which would make them a unified fighting force again. Out on the flanks of the half circle bridgehead infantry fought ahead in comparatively small groups.

Resistance was light at first but during the night it was reported that two large German convoys were racing full speed for the American bridgehead with all their lights full on.

The bridgehead, however, is secure and the greatest break of the war, the Ludendorff bridge, has been exploited perfectly.

Rhine Bridge Nazi Gift to Ninth Armd., by Andy Rooney, Stars and Stripes staff writer.

Ten

The Bridge at Remagen

T he following story comes from a booklet printed in Bayreuth, Germany, entitled simply *The Bridge:*

Story of the Crossing That Startled the World

The Ninth Armored Division attained the pinnacle of fame on March 7, 1945, by unexpectedly establishing the first allied bridgehead over the Rhine. All the united nations cheered this daring triumph.

By seizing intact the old Ludendorff railroad bridge at Remagen and quickly crossing to the east bank of the Rhine, the Ninth Armored Division opened up immense military possibilities that were realized to the fullest when it came time for the allied armies to drive farther into Germany.

No other military event in Europe, excepting perhaps the D day landings in Normandy, so stirred the popular imagination. An avalanche of new stories and broadcasts poured out of the bridgehead area. The Ninth Armored soon became one of the most highly publicized American divisions in history.

Capture of the Remagen bridge climaxed a swift dash by the Ninth Armored's commands from the Roer River to the Rhine. Combat Command B took off from the Roer on February 28, Combat Command A the following day. Combat Command R was in reserve.

Combat Command B and Combat Command A, advancing in coordinated movements, were ready March 6 for the final plunge to the Rhine.

At this point, the possibility suggested itself that the Ninth Armored might drive swiftly to the south and establish contact on the Rhine with units of the Third Army. A rapid link-up with Third Army forces would mean the trapping of perhaps thousands of Germans on the west bank of the Rhine.

Combat Command B was given the mission of taking the towns of Remagen, Kripp, and Sinzig and securing crossings of the Ahr River at

Sinzig and Bodendorf. In addition, CCB was to clear the enemy from the zone west of the Rhine. Combat Command A was to seize Bad Neuenahr, a famous German resort town not far from the Rhine, and secure crossings over the Ahr in the Bad Neuenahr-Hiemersheim sector.

Major General John W. Leonard, commanding general of the Ninth Armored, conferred with Brigadier General William M. Hoge, commanding general of Combat Command B, at Stadt Meckenheim on the morning of March 7. They decided that if the Remagen bridge were found intact, CCB would send troops across and establish a bridgehead on the east bank of the Rhine.

CCB columns were already on the move toward the Rhine. The North task force was commanded by Lieutenant Colonel Leonard E. Engeman of the 14th Tank Battalion, whose mission was to take Remagen and Kripp. The force was composed of the 14th Tank Battalion, less B Company, the 27th Armored Infantry Battalion commanded by Major Murray Deevers, and one platoon of C Troop of the 89th Cavalry Reconnaissance Squadron, Mechanized.

The South column had the mission of capturing the Ahr bridges at Bodendorf and Sinzig and establishing a bridgehead south of the Ahr at Sinzig. This task force included C Troop of the 89th, less one platoon; the 52nd Armored Infantry Battalion, commanded by Lieutenant Colonel William R. Prince; Company B of the 14th Tank Battalion; one platoon of Company B, 9th Armored Engineer Battalion; and one platoon of Company C, 656th Tank Destroyer Battalion.

Combat Command B's reserve was composed of Headquarters CCB, plus a 78th Infantry Division unit, the 1st Battalion of the 310th Infantry, which was attached to the 9th Armored Division; Company B of the 9th Armored Engineers, less one platoon; and Company C of the 656th TDs [Tank Destroyers].

Major Ben Cothran carried the instructions about the Remagen bridge to the commander of the North task force, Colonel Engeman.

When Colonel Engeman came out on the high hill overlooking the Rhine at Remagen, he saw through his binoculars that German vehicles were still fleeing over the bridge to the east.

Colonel Engeman immediately sent a platoon of the new Pershing 90mm tanks down the winding road into Remagen. The tanks, from Company A of the 14th Tank Battalion, were commanded by First Lieutenant John Grimball. Following the tanks were dismounted troops of Company A of the 27th Armored Infantry Battalion. Their empty half-tracks brought up the rear.

While these forces were fighting their way through Remagen,

information was obtained from a prisoner of war taken inside the town and from a civilian questioned by the 52nd Armored Infantry Battalion at Sinzig that the bridge was scheduled to be blown at 1600 [4 p.m.]. These reports were sent to General Hoge. The time was 1515 [3:15 p.m.]. He immediately sent a message to Colonel Engeman that he had 45 minutes to take the bridge.

The dash to the Rhine was accelerated. Colonel Engeman, wishing to check on the progress of his platoon of tanks, radio-telephoned the following message to Lieutenant Grimball: "Get to the bridge as rapidly as possible."

This reply came back from Lieutenant Grimball, a South Carolinian: "Suh, I am already there."

Grimball's tanks took up firing positions near the bridge. When the 27th's Company A raced up to the west end of the bridge, the time was 1550, ten minutes before the hour for touching off the explosives.

But the Germans, in the face of the onrushing Ninth Armored troops, frantically began trying to destroy the bridge before the time set.

The enemy set off two charges.

One charge blew a crater in the western approaches to the bridge on the roadway. The second blast, which was touched off just as the 27th's men were starting across, occurred about two-thirds of the way across the bridge. The second explosion knocked out one of the principal diagonal supports on the upstream side of the main arch. It destroyed a section of the bridge flooring and left a 6-inch sag at the damaged pier point.

The cap went off on a 500-pound TNT charge set up with time fuses near the north railing, also about two-thirds of the way across, but that charge failed to explode.

As the men of the 27th dashed across, they were getting covering fire from the platoon of Pershing tanks drawn up around the west end of the span. Despite the threat of recurring blasts, the infantrymen kept going. The first platoon of Company A was in front. Following were the third and second platoons. The men were fully aware that they had only ten minutes, and they felt the bridge might be blown at any time.

Three members of the Ninth Armored Engineer Battalion hurried onto the bridge to prevent the Germans, if possible, from setting off any further explosions. They were First Lieutenant Hugh Mott, Staff Sergeant John Reynolds, and Sergeant Eugene Dorland. The engineers rapidly cut all the wires connected to 40-pound charges below deck. Then they sped across the bridge to cut the main cable. The cable would not yield to the pair of small pliers carried by Dorland, so he fired three shots into it from his carbine, smashing the main hook-up.

LIEGE EDITION

1st THE STARS AND STRIPES

Daily News paper of U.S. Armed Forces   in the European Theater of Operations
Vol. I—No. 49   Friday, March 9, 1945

Ici On Parle Français

Il pleuvra demain.
Eel pluvra duh-man.
It will rain tomorrow.

ARMY ACROSS RHINE

Victory, Nazi Shells in Air On Pay-Dirt Side of Rhine

By Chris Cunningham
United Press War Correspondent

ON THE EAST BANK OF THE RHINE, Mar. 8 —"Hell," the officer said, "if you have something given to you the best thing is to take it."

He was talking over here on this "pay dirt" side. Shells were hitting all around, but there was victory in the air—as if it spelled the beginning of the end.

It was the question of a quick decision on the part of a second lieutenant named Emmet J. Burrows and his A Company.

For security reasons, this correspondent is unable to tell how it was done. But judging from the way the Germans are throwing in some of their heaviest stuff at us tonight, they surely know when, where, how and why we got across the Rhine.

In a short time we got across. The time was 3:50 PM yesterday (Wednesday). The outfit that got over here had orders to seize any opportunities for crossing that it could. From the company commander on up to the battalion commander to the division commander to the corps commander, the word went that we could cross.

Without a moment's hesitation, the entire company got across, and tonight their bridgehead is rapidly expanding both eastward, to the north and to the south. It reminds me a great deal of the Anzio beachhead in Italy, only this time there isn't even the threat of our getting kicked out of it.

The place where this outfit crossed the Rhine is one of the most picturesque spots south of Cologne. As a matter of fact, the only reason that we got across was that the Germans got caught nappi by the outfit that took it on the chin during the Belgian bulge. It now
(Continued on Page 4)

Forges Bridgehead South of Cologne In Surprise Move

By Dan Regan
Stars and Stripes Staff Writer

WITH FIRST U.S. ARMY, Mar. 8.—First Army troops have crossed the Rhine River south of Cologne and have established a bridgehead on the east bank.

After a surprise move at 1640 hours yesterday, Lt. Gen. Courtney H. Hodges' men struck across the last great water barrier to the heart of Germany, apparently hitting the Germans where they least expected it. For the past several days German opposition has been completely disorganized, and a news blackout had been imposed on American operations.

(Meanwhile, Associated Press reported from Supreme Allied Headquarters that a temporary news blackout had dropped over the last gap —well under 25 miles— separating the First Army from Lt. Gen. George S. Patton's Third U.S. Army spearheads, which reached the Rhine north of Coblenz Wednesday.)

There was enough explosive on the bridge to destroy even a much larger structure.

The infantrymen, meanwhile, were getting in their licks. The bridge crackled with battle. German machine gunners were spraying the Americans from the tower on the bridge. Technical Sergeant Joseph Delisio captured two men at one gun; Technical Sergeant Mike Chinchar took care of the other gun. While the two Americans were in the towers, their men raced on across. Sergeant Alexander Drabik was the first man to cross the Rhine.

As the men reached the east end of the bridge, some veered to the left and others moved straight ahead into a railroad tunnel, to clean it out.

After the crossing came the Battle of Flak Hill. Lieutenant Emmet Burrows took his second platoon up the sheer cliff above the eastern bank. For several hours these men, along with others of the 27th, held the Remagen bridgehead.

It was rugged going for Burrows and his men. Besides their rifles and carbines, they had one machine gun. They clung to roots on the hill while the Germans shot down at them. The enemy troops tried to dislodge them by rolling rocks down the face of the cliff.

New York World-Telegram

Copyright, 1945, by New York World-Telegram Corporation. All rights reserved.

Local Forecast: Tonight mostly clear. Tomorrow partly cloudy and mild.

VOL. 77—NO. 209—IN TWO SECTIONS—SECTION ONE.   NEW YORK, FRIDAY, MARCH 9, 1945   Entered as second class matter Post Office, New York, N. Y.

CLOSING WALL ST.

Five Cents

YANKS SWARMING OVER CAPTURED RHINE BRIDGE

Arc 5 Mi. Deep, 10 Wide; Berlin Battle in Full Fury

By BRUCE W. MUNN, *United Press War Correspondent.*

PARIS, March 9.—Powerful armored and infantry forces of the American 1st Army steadily expanded the solid bridgehead across the Rhine from Remagen today.

[The Associated Press said the east bank wedge had now grown to at least **five miles** deep and 10 miles—possibly more—wide.]

The security blackout that had cloaked the progress of the 1st Army since it broke across the Rhine 48 hours ago was lifted dramatically today to reveal that the Ludendorff Bridge had been captured intact in probably the most amazing military coup of the war.

While the men hung on, a German flak wagon in the rear opened up on them with four 20mm guns. One man fell to his death on a rock ledge far below the summit of the cliff.

But still they stayed there until they were relieved after dark. That kind of fighting spirit characterized the entire Remagen bridgehead battle.

With one of the most significant operations of the European War in full swing, an unexpected development threatened to upset its exploitation. General Hoge was pursuing his advantage to the utmost when a ticklish command problem arose. While he was pushing his troops across the bridge, orders were received from III Corps for the Ninth Armored to move south across the Ahr River and drive down the west bank of the Rhine. Ninth Armored troops already were on the east bank, but word of the crossing had not yet reached III Corps.

As a result of the new orders, General Hoge issued directions for the troops who had crossed the bridge to remain in their present positions until he could obtain further instructions from General Leonard.

General Leonard quickly made a bold decision that later won him the plaudits of high allied commanders. He was fully cognizant of the dangers involved. There was the possibility of a German trap on the other side of the river. The enemy might wait until CCB had sent most of its troops across the river, then counterattack in such force as to destroy our bridgehead and the men in it. No one knew for certain the strength of the Germans on the east side of the Rhine opposite Remagen.

New York World-Telegram

Copyright 1945, by New York World-Telegram Corporation. All rights reserved.

Local Forecast: Partly cloudy this afternoon and tonight. Tomorrow fair.

VOL. 77—NO. 210—IN TWO SECTIONS—SECTION ONE.　　NEW YORK, SATURDAY, MARCH 10, 1945

LATEST
WALL ST.
PRICES

Five Cents

YANKS BEAT OFF BLOW AT RHINE BRIDGEHEAD

Blocks in Flames

PalaceGrounds Seared in Raid By 300 B-29s

15 Square Miles Of City Called

Reds Hammer Way Into Stettin Suburbs

By ROBERT MUSEL
United Press Staff Correspondent

LONDON, March 10 —Soviet troops and tanks were reported battling today through the streets of Altdamm...

1st and 3rd Rounding Up 50,000 Germans Cut Off In the Eifel Mountains

By BRUCE W. MUNN,
United Press War Correspondent.

PARIS, March 10.—Reinforced American 1st Army troops beat off weak German counterblows against their deepening Rhine bridgehead today and joined with U. S. 3rd Army forces west of the river in a mass roundup of perhaps 50,000 Germans trapped in the Eifel Mountains.

[The Associated Press said tank-supported German infantry struck at the bridgehead as more thousands of doughboys sped over the bridge in a race against Nazi columns moving up for battle. So massive was U. S. power rolling across the Ludendorff Bridge that a front correspondent declared the Germans already have lost the race.]

(Radio Paris broadcast an unconfirmed but possibly...

General Leonard also weighed the possibility that the enemy might be able to destroy the bridge soon after the Ninth Armored went across, leaving his troops high and dry on the other side of the Rhine, perhaps at the mercy of strong German forces. There were German airfields nearby. And a lucky artillery hit might knock out the bridge.

Despite all the risks inherent in the situation, General Leonard instructed General Hoge to go ahead and expand the bridgehead while he contacted III Corps Headquarters. He assured General Hoge that he would relieve all CCB troops on the western side of the river at once, leaving General Hoge free to handle the bridgehead with all the troops at his disposal. General Leonard said he would have Combat Command A relieve Combat Command B's South column at Sinzig.

He also would have the 89th Cavalry Squadron relieve the 1st Battalion of the 310th Infantry on the north.

General Hoge arranged to employ these forces across the river. He now was in position to capitalize on the great prize that had been won by the daring and initiative of troops under his command.

When III Corps was informed of the Rhine crossing, General Leonard's orders were confirmed, and the order was full speed ahead on the bridgehead. Combat Command A was directed to hold the bridgehead over the Ahr River. The Ninth Armored's mission to the south was modified.

In the inky darkness of that first night on the bridge, tanks of Company A, 14th Tank Battalion, began to move across the bridge. Military vehicles headed toward Remagen from almost all points in the area, and traffic snarls developed.

One unfortunate incident occurred in the darkness to complicate the problems of getting armor into the bridgehead. A tank destroyer of the 656th TD Battalion slipped off the bridge roadway and was perched precariously on two beams, unable to use its own power. Herculean efforts were launched to remove the TD, and all vehicular traffic on the bridge had to be halted. The TD, which had slipped through the unstable flooring, finally was towed safely off the bridge. Armored infantry battalions, meanwhile, had been leaving their vehicles in Remagen and crossing the bridge on foot.

Enemy reaction to the Ninth Armored's seizure of the Remagen bridge was extremely violent. The Germans counterattacked savagely with tanks and infantry as soon as they could wheel into position. They hurled a storm of artillery fire and bombs at the bridgehead. Veterans compared it to the hell of Normandy.

Hundreds of Luftwaffe pilots were sent on suicide missions to get the bridge. The 482nd Anti-Aircraft Battalion protected the bridge alone at the outset and shot down the first four German planes that flew over the span. The 482nd later was joined by a massive concentration of antiaircraft weapons. The German fliers, pursuing their reckless tactics, were able to obtain hits and near-hits on the bridge, but they were not enough.

The Germans sent mines floating down the river, hoping they would hit the railroad bridge or the pontoon structures that were being thrown across. They sent men down the river on barges loaded with explosives. They even tried specially trained swimmers who paddled down the river in rubber suits towing heavy charges of floating explosives.

For ten days the Ludendorff bridge withstood all enemy action. Heavy military traffic poured across. After the bridge virtually had served its usefulness to the allied cause, it toppled into the Rhine.

In the ten days that the railroad bridge had been in our hands, several pontoon bridges across the Rhine had been completed. There was no immediate further need for the Ludendorff span.

* * *

We were ordered to Bad Neuenahr, and orders were given simultaneously that every gun would be fired at planes in order to put as many bullets as possible in the air when aircraft flew over. One fellow sat down with the stock of his carbine on the ground and just pumped the bullets from it. He remarked that he had just as good a chance of hitting

Two views of a Cologne Cathedral.

the planes as those who were aiming. In the beginning, this was all right, but as antiaircraft units would arrive, they would continually increase the firepower of the units on the ground. The old saying, "Whatever goes up must come down" certainly was true about the shrapnel and bullets.

According to notes I made at the time, fifteen battalions of antiaircraft were assigned to CCB, and these battalions took up positions in the valley around the bridge. Later, however, space was at a premium, and they set up wherever they could find room — whether in the valley or on top of a hill. Most of the days were heavily overcast, and the enemy planes would stay above the overcast for a while. The high-level antiaircraft guns, with radar, would be firing, and this would be taking place above the clouds. At the same time, the German pilots were dropping Christmas tinsel from their planes, which would upset the radar. It looked like Christmas in some areas, with tinsel hanging from all of the trees.

When a plane would plunge through the clouds and became visible to the gunners below, the area would explode into action. There were so many guns on all areas of the hills that when the German aircraft were able to get low enough to go between the hills, the crossfire would be terrific.

Bad Neuenahr was a resort town, so we started looking around for some of the area's finer beverages. I went down into one cellar and was stunned to see endless rows of 500-gallon barrels. These barrels were so large that I could not even see over the top of them, so I stepped up on a spigot on one of the barrels and looked around. When I used my flashlight, the beam showed barrel after barrel in deep rows, and my light just disappeared into the dark, without even hitting a back wall. I figured I had found the largest supply in all of Germany. But just then a voice said, "All right, everybody out of here." Since he and I were the only two in there, I presumed he was speaking to me. I responded by asking him who he was to be giving orders. He said he was "Military Government," which meant nothing to me. He again ordered me out, and I replied that I had come in for something and intended to go out with something. I guess he decided that diplomacy was the best policy, because he then said, "All right, take what you want but don't tell any of your friends or come back for more." Needless to say, when I left there, our crew was well supplied. Frankly, I figured that Military Government was just seizing all that alcohol to make sure the officers would have their monthly ration. That was all right with me — as long as we got ours first.

One time, I was working on the radio when one of the fellows reached into the back door of the half-track and handed me a bottle of wine, saying that it was great stuff and I should try it. I was very busy sending and receiving, but I opened the bottle and sipped it as time went by. When my relief came, I stepped down from the half-track and almost went on my ear. I had sipped away that whole bottle and didn't have a leg under me.

We received orders from SHEAF that any man caught drunk while on duty would be court-martialed. This made a big hit with our company. One of the fellows had been a master of ceremonies with a night club in New York and his routine when something like this: "They are threatening me with dire consequences if I drink. If I am caught drunk I will be court-martialed. The Germans are trying to maim or kill me and they are going to take me away from all this. I will be court-martialed and sent back to the States where I will be safe. Where's the bottle?" We really thought that order was hilarious.

Jim Shaughnessy, one of our messengers, was ordered to deliver a message over the bridge. Getting across was no problem, as all traffic was eastbound. When it came time to return, however, the vehicle had no priority to cross the bridge; the only priority westbound was for ambulances. So he went down along the river and found a boat. He abandoned his Jeep on the east side of the river, rowed across the Rhine, and returned to the company. Snipers were an extra spur to his efforts in rowing the boat.

One fairly clear day, a plane was high up and the high-level antiaircraft was firing. I didn't recognize the outline of the plane, but I wasn't very good at that sort of thing anyway. Off in the distance, I could see six P-38s approaching, and I figured it would be interesting to watch a dogfight. I was amazed that the German pilot seemed unaware of the approaching aircraft. Finally, when they were almost together, the German plane just wheeled and was gone. I couldn't believe what had happened. This was the first jet aircraft that I had ever seen, and I didn't know what it was. Thankfully, the Germans didn't get a chance to develop those in any quantity.

We were taught to lead aircraft by five planelengths when firing at them, and one day when an observation plane flew over us, I opened fire. He just ignored what I was doing until I happened to realize that this fellow wasn't traveling at the speed of a fighter. I cut my lead down to almost nothing, and all of a sudden he left. There were others firing also, but maybe we began to get a little close.

As I remember, 110 enemy aircraft were shot down over the bridge. But planes were not the only method of airborne attack that the Germans used. Once I was in a hotel building not far from the bridge when suddenly I felt like a giant hand had picked me up and thrown me face-first into the wall. I fell to the floor stunned, picked myself up, and, in a confused state, groped for my helmet and rifle. I figured the building was coming down around my ears. I raced outside in time to see a huge column of dirt and debris gradually settling to the ground on a ridge about a quarter of a mile away. The Germans had fired a V-2 rocket at the bridge, but at that time they could not project them with any great accuracy. I had never before (or have since) taken a wallop like that.

From the time the bridge was taken, canisters of smoke were used to envelop that area and conceal not only the bridge itself but also such activity as the deployment of pontoon bridges. How they were able to hold pontoon bridges on a river that wide with such strong current is beyond my comprehension. Three bridges were being put across the river so we would not have to rely on the Remagen bridge. The smoke was covering all these efforts.

My brother Dick was with the 29th Infantry Division, and I read in Stars and Stripes that the 29th was across the river from Dusseldorf, about a hundred miles north of the bridge. Since it was obvious that we would be digging in for a while, I asked if I could have a forty-eight-hour pass to visit him, and that was granted. Hitching a ride was no problem,

because GIs would always pick up other GIs heading in the direction they were going.

I reached Cologne very quickly, but then I encountered a minor problem. The dividing line between the First Army and the Ninth Army was just north of Cologne, and there was no intermingling of traffic. Finally, a truck driver agreed to give me a lift to where I could pick up a Ninth Army vehicle. In the Ninth Army sector, another truck driver came along and picked me up. He started to question me about where I had come from, so I told him. Then he asked me if I had the password. I told him I did, but I gave him the challenge from the First Army. He laughed and said that when you change armies, you also change passwords, so even though he knew nothing about me, he told me both the challenge and the response for the Ninth Army. He then asked me which way I would like to travel northward, since there was a fast way and a slow way. I responded that he was driving, and I would go whatever way suited him. He then told me that he liked to travel the fast way along the Rhine because there was no traffic along the river, but occasionally the Germans would take a crack at him. We went the fast way.

Left to right: Dick and I meet across the Rhine from Dusseldorf. We are indicating that he has one stripe and I have three.

When we arrived at the area where he was to drop me off, I was reminded that units always operated under code names. Nobody could tell me where the 29th Infantry was billeted, but finally one GI told me that my best bet would be to go into the basement of a factory on the edge of town and to ask there. When I arrived at the factory, it was a beehive of activity. It obviously was a command post, with maps pinned to all the walls and everyone extremely busy. Since nobody was paying any attention to me, I started to look at the maps, trying to locate my brother's outfit. Suddenly I heard, "Who the hell are you?" I turned to find a major glaring at me. He put me through the usual questioning on my dog tags, asked where I was from, etc. Finally, he looked at me and said, "I'll see that you get to your destination." He called for MPs, and when they arrived, he ordered, "Take this guy to the 29th Infantry and make G-d- sure he has a brother in that outfit."

I jumped in the Jeep, delighted that I was being given special transportation to my brother's outfit. When we arrived, the company clerk advised us that there was no McAvoy with that company. I was shocked. When I asked about casualties and transfers, he remarked that a group had recently been transferred to a field-artillery outfit, and he would look it up. I stood there thinking of that spy we had caught in the Roer Valley and hoping that my trial might last a little longer than his did.

The clerk returned with the welcome news that my brother had been transferred to that outfit, and it was only a short distance away. The MPs took me right to the company, and Dick and I met for the first time in a few years. He had been with the 29th Infantry during the D day landings at Normandy.

I stayed overnight with him at his company's bivouac area and ate with him at the company mess. We had a great visit, and he made arrangements for me to get a ride out of there the following morning.

Bonn, Germany, just south of Cologne. (Right) Rhine River looking south. Large hill on left provided fair protection from attacks by 88s.

The ride got me as far as Cologne, and somehow I happened onto an airport. There I was advised that an observation plane from my division would be coming in at 5 o'clock, and the pilot would love to have someone ride with him. They convinced me, so I waited for the plane to come in. When it arrived, the pilot had his mechanic with him, and they could not take me. He had gotten so fed up with flying alone that he had talked his mechanic into making the trip. So now it was already five o'clock, and I still had a long way to go. Luckily enough, all traffic was headed toward the bridge, so I had no trouble getting a ride that far. When I arrived at the bridge, it was pitch dark, and they had just taken some hits. An MP told me that he would get me a ride, but I could see that he was pretty keyed up — he had been evacuating wounded. Naturally, since all vehicles were traveling with blackout lights, I would only get a ride if the MP would place me on a vehicle. We lay in a doorway, and I suspect that he could have gotten me a ride even sooner than he did, except that he wanted company. Finally, there was a vehicle going to my company, and I got back in the wee hours of the morning. I would never do anything like that again.

When we were at Camp Polk, one of our buddies broke his ankle in a ball game and was transferred to another outfit, and we left without him. Now we heard that his outfit was arriving at the bridge, and some of us went there to meet him. In a way, it was kind of comical. When his battalion arrived, we asked where his company was located. They were crossing single file, and they told us it was to the rear. We kept asking for his company until the last company of that battalion arrived. Again we asked for him, and they just kept pointing to the rear. The very last man of that company to arrive was our friend — the very last man of the battalion. It was great seeing him again, and a strange place for a reunion.

Rheinbrohl, Germany, looking north and west. The hill with the houses was crawling with antiaircraft.

Rhine River, Rheinbrohl, Germany, March 1945. East bank looking west. 78th Infantry Division is on other side waiting to cross over.

Eleven

Ninth Armored in on the Kill

As the 9th Armored Division wheeled south along the Rhine, the long-hailed combined operations began in the north. General Omar Bradley's remark that the First Army could break from the Remagen bridgehead any time it chose seemed to be the signal for the big push. Combat Command B suddenly turned east in a lightning advance.

Racing over rugged terrain, CCB's tanks hit the Autobahn leading toward Limburg, hooking up with the 7th Armored Division's tanks. Armor of both divisions sped abreast down the wide highway until the 7th was ordered to shift directly east. When tanks of CCB's 19th Battalion reached Limburg, the armor immediately darted across the bridge over the Lahn River. Three tanks got across. A fourth was on the span when the Germans set off charges. The tank teetered on the far brink, then slowly pulled onto the far side. However, these tanks were now cut off, and the Nazis attacked savagely with bazookas.

The tankmen were rescued when Company C, 52nd Armored Infantry Battalion, threw a makeshift bridge across the river, and infantrymen fought their way into Limburg.

Capture of the city was highly significant. Not only did it mark the complete breakout of the Remagen bridgehead, but it was the forerunner of swift armored advances across central Germany that put American forces in position to help seal off the industrial Ruhr Valley.

The first German prison camp was captured at Limburg, and its occupants were liberated. According to the booklet The 9th, General Leonard visited a Limburg hospital and met patients who had been former members of the division. "You are in good hands now," he encouraged them.

When we broke out of the Remagen bridgehead, we moved out of Bad Neuenahr, crossed the Rhine on one of the pontoon bridges, and entered the town of Rhinebrohl. It was here that one member of our company had relatives, and he went looking for them. This fellow was Pennsylvania Dutch, and he spoke that comic, guttural German that I thought was just for fun and the movies. I was amazed that these people refused to believe that he had never been in Germany before — they thought he was a native. His German was a strong provincial dialect.

First 50 Mi.

Wednesday, March 28, 1945

Beyond Rhine

2 Armored Forces Speed Eastward; Doughs Meet Third

Two armored spearheads of the First U.S. Army rolled almost 36 miles farther into Germany yesterday, and last night they were 50 miles east of the Rhine in the deepest announced penetration into Germany from the West. At the same time, it was reported that the First and Third Armies joined east of the Rhine in the vicinity of Lahnstein, southeast of Coblenz, where unidentified forces of the First met the Third's 87th Inf. Div.

To the southeast, Third Army tanks smashed into Bavaria, in southern Germany, across the Main River, but a news blackout screened their progress. They were last reported 40 miles beyond the Rhine in the Aschaffenberg area.

Ninth Is Counter-Attacked

Above the Ruhr, in the Ninth U.S. Army sector, the Americans held a bridgehead 14 miles deep, but progress was slowed temporarily yesterday as the first counter-attack since the crossing was reported from the 30th Inf. Div.'s front.

Just north of Mannheim, at the southern end of the Rhine front, the Seventh U.S. Army had a bridgehead 19 miles long and four miles deep.

The First Army tanks which burst out from the Remagen bridgehead were facing only light resistance. One column reached the vicinity of Herborn, 50 miles east of Bad Godesberg on the Rhine as another armored tip reached a point two miles north of Wetzlar, about the same distance from the river.

Wetzlar is the home of the Leica camera factory.

Tanks Near Wiesbaden

It was disclosed yesterday that the Ninth Armd. and Second Inf. Divs. are participating in what was described as "the First Army's Berlin drive."

Ninth Armd. spearheads rolled 21 miles southeast of Limburg to reach a point five miles southeast of Wiesbaden, just north of Mainz.

Hundreds of First Army tanks—one of the greatest armored forces ever assembled—rolled through Germany, by-passing unimportant towns. Motorized infantry followed close behind for mopping up operations. Behind them came the old fashioned doughfeet, who took care of the final cleanup.

A common sight.

A temporary grave.

What amazed me was that probably ninety percent of the people had fled the town, but his relative happened to be one of the ten percent who had remained.

That night, the firing was so severe that the ground was bucking incredibly, and it was impossible to lie down and try to sleep. Finally, I threw my bedroll up on the hood of the half-track and let the vehicle take the shocks, so I was able to get a very uncomfortable night's sleep. Armor plate is not the softest bedding.

The next night, I found a small barn with a manger that had six-inch-thick concrete walls for stalls. The walls were about three feet high, and the manger was covered with hay. I curled up in a corner and went to sleep. The shelling that night was intense, and when I awoke in the morning, the manger was full to overflowing with men who had taken refuge. Obviously, I had chosen an excellent place to sleep.

The 9th continued the story:

"Ninth Armored combat commands next raced in two directions. While CCB and CCA made a record advance to the north, CCR dashed south along the autobahn to link up with Third Army forces near Niederhausen. [This drive was to ensure a successful Rhine crossing by the Third Army near Frankfurt.]

"CCB covered 67 miles one day during the drive to the north. CCA advanced 70 miles in 11 hours. German troops surrendered in droves. CCA alone took more than 1200 PWs March 29th.

"Considerable resistance was encountered at Fritzlar, site of a large German airport. CCA captured 15 planes and another aircraft was shot down by Corporal Odus C. Todd, Eubank, Kentucky, 14th Tank Battalion. A round from Todd's 76mm struck the plane in the tail assembly, promptly bringing it down.

"The 9th's advance to the north helped complete the encirclement of the Ruhr. German forces struck at the steel ring in the Warburg area, but few succeeded in escaping. CCB beat off a strong counterattack near Bonenberg, April 2. Germans hurled 250 infantrymen and from three to five tanks at the town.

"CCB sent reinforcements and a large number of the enemy was caught in the open by artillery fire and direct fire from tanks. The Nazis withdrew after suffering heavy casualties.

"The number of prisoners ultimately taken from the Ruhr pocket far

Remagen Span 3 Minutes After Fall

This is the first picture taken of the Ludendorf bridge after it crashed into the Rhine Saturday afternoon. It was taken, less than three minutes after the span collapsed, by 1/Lt. Marcus Hoffman, of San Francisco, from the Remagen end of the bridge.

While the collapse came without warning, there was no traffic on the bridge at the time.

First Army engineers on the scene believe that constant traffic, combined with several German artillery hits had so weakened the bridge that it could no longer support its own weight.

The great center span swayed, then twisted slightly. Then the western end of the span fell from the mid-river pier, pulling both end sections from the east and west banks.

A large number of men from an engineer battalion were dumped into the river and were buried under the twisted girders.

The center section between the two piers off shore disappeared into the water. The end sections broke and formed crooked Vs between their piers and the towers at their shore ends.

Remagen Span Collapses, Weakened by Shell Hits

By Andy Rooney
Stars and Stripes Staff Writer

REMAGEN, Mar. 18—The Ludendorf bridge crumpled into the Rhine yesterday afternoon, ten days to the hour after the Ninth Armored Div. captured it and crossed the River.

Andy Rooney's story.

exceeded the total anticipated. Altogether, the Allies captured 327,000. This was the first great dividend of the Remagen bridgehead. General Eisenhower commended all forces involved in the Ruhr operation: 'This victory of allied arms is a fitting prelude to the final battle to crush the ragged remnants of Hitler's armies of the west, now tottering on the threshold of defeat.' "

* * *

Left to right: Gen. Leonard, Col. Lusk, and McAvoy—Delivers message during Leipzig Drive. (Acme News Photo, Toledo Times)

Limburg was the most emotional point of the war for us. During World War II, when you lost men, there never was any word of what had happened to them unless you had correspondence with the family — and most of us didn't. In the Battle of the Bulge, men had disappeared. Suddenly, in Limburg, we had opened up a prison camp and released 2,600 American prisoners — our own guys. Not just Americans, but some of the men we had lost. We were horrified at their condition. When we last saw them, they were strong, strapping young fellows of 160 to 180 pounds, and here were our buddies weighing approximately seventy-five to eighty pounds, with sunken eyes, hollow cheeks, and protruding teeth. It was a terrible shock, yet also a joyous moment. Our own buddies even came and found us. When our troops captured the city and released the prisoners, they immediately recognized the patches the troops were wearing. They asked where they could find our company, and eventually they were successful.

Unfortunately, we were young and untrained for anything like this. Our first thoughts were that these men were starving to death, and we

A calf's thigh bone with
nuts and bolts through it
— used as a whip on
forced labor of Germany.

needed to feed them. I carried two chocolate bars, 900 calories each, in the front pockets of my field jacket. (I always swore that the chocolate was so hard that no bullet could penetrate it.) We gave these men chocolate, plus C-rations, K-rations, and cans of American cheese (1,000 calories). Most of the men became deathly ill from the shock to their systems of getting this much nourishment. They had been existing on about 100 calories a day, mainly a weak soup. When we were ordered to move on, we almost rebelled. Then someone mentioned that we had done about as much damage as possible with our ignorance, and these fellows would be better off getting some professional assistance. So we took an emotional leave of them.

We arrived at a high-level bridge that had been blown away on the left side, and the right side sagged to such an extent that a Jeep in front of us carrying four men disappeared into the sag — even though we were standing in the half-track. The bridge was probably eight to ten stories above the ground. A young engineer was directing the vehicles one at a time, and our ten-ton half-track was next. One of our fellows asked this young fellow whether the bridge was safe, and his response was, "We haven't lost anyone yet." We gingerly crossed that span, and the whole column behind us did too.

We arrived at a crossroad that the air corps had been bombing in

Advancing toward Leipzig. Colored panel on top of trailer is air identification code so friendly aircraft would not strafe us.

Delaying actions of blown bridges.

Stopped by an enemy roadblock — always maintaining distance. Round bar at bottom of picture is our bazooka.

front of us, and a 500-pound bomb had made a dead-center hit on the crossroad but had not exploded. We gingerly passed that bomb — which was buried in the pavement up to its fins — hoping that the vibration of our vehicle would not trigger it.

We now broke out of Limburg and started an advance that was to be both frustrating and exhilarating. We ran off the maps that were being supplied to us, because we were moving more rapidly than expected. A plane landed beside us on the Reichsautobahn, the German superhighway, carrying detailed maps for an area we had passed ten miles back. We then began looting houses for road maps — anything we could find to help us. Of course, the maps we found were in German, so this created another problem: There were major differences in spelling. For example, Cologne was Köln, Munich was München, and Prague was Praha. Our orders were to move ahead to certain areas, but we had to do it with these seized German maps.

As we moved forward, the Luftwaffe attempted to strafe and bomb our columns. A plane would come in so fast that very few of us would open fire on the first pass. Then the pilot would make what I considered to be a major mistake: He would soar up and take a huge turn to make another run on the column. Every vehicle was armed with at least one machine gun — up to the multiple .50-caliber antiaircraft machine guns and pom-poms — so we would be prepared for his second run. Every gunner was in position, and when he started his second pass, he met a hail of fire. I don't remember any plane making a second run and getting away from us. Sometimes we would be in small towns when the strafing attack would come, and we would follow him down until we were taking the roofs off the houses with our fire. I can remember slate shingles flying in the air as we followed them down. Since there was only one machine gun on our vehicle, the man on the gun would be doing the firing, assisted by one of us. The rest would be spectators.

The Germans in the towns were advised to hang anything white out of the windows of their homes if they intended to surrender without a fight. In some towns, it looked like all the wash in town was on the lines — with sheets, pillowcases, towels, and anything else white hanging from all the windows and poles. But we entered one town that was liberally displaying the white flag when suddenly they opened up on us. Two of our men were killed in this violation of the white truce flag. We took some prisoners in order to find out which officer had ordered the Germans to open fire. There was a group of about a dozen prisoners lined up, and our men were pulling the necks of their jackets down to expose the underside of the left armpit — the location of the brand on an SS man. We would look down the line, and we could see that the Volkstrom were very curious about what was taking place. The looks on their faces were enough. Then, beyond the Volkstrom would be a German standing stiffly and showing no curiosity, and we knew that was an SS. They were questioned and refused to answer at first, but it didn't take long before they were willing to explain why some of our buddies had been murdered. They rapidly — and noticeably — changed their tune. It developed that an SS captain had demanded that they hold their fire until our men had entered the town and then open up, despite the white flags. The rules of warfare are in the eyes of the beholder. Once all of the information had been obtained, the armored field artillery was called in to destroy the town as a lesson for any other town that might attempt to use the white flag to lure our men into an ambush. When ordered to do this, the field-artillery officer shrugged and said, "We have nothing else to do." (When an armored unit is moving rapidly, there is little for the field artillery to do but follow and help to mop up.)

We were accompanied by four British commandos, who would travel with us during the day and then, when we would stop for the night, they would take over. They had a Jeep with a twin Vickers machine gun on it, and they pulled a trailer with a huge searchlight. After dark, the four of them would advance up the road and get around behind the Germans.

Bridges were almost always blown to try to delay us.

While we slept, they would intermittently use that searchlight to expose positions and then fire on the enemy with the machine gun. They would stay in behind the lines for only a short period — just enough to make the Germans nervous for the rest of the night.

As we advanced, we opened fire on a group of Germans whom we spotted on the edge of a forest. When they surrendered, we signaled them to walk toward us. After we disarmed them, we smashed their weapons against the steel-plate corners of the half-track. Then we told them to start walking, since we could not be bogged down with prisoners. They started to walk back along the road the way we had come, and some of them would walk backward, facing us, fearing we would gun them down. It was really the decision of the man on the machine gun as to whether or not to fire. The massacre of our men who had surrendered during the Battle of the Bulge, plus the condition of the ones freed at Limburg, was still foremost in our minds. I often wondered how far they walked before they were actually taken prisoner. At that time, we were deep behind enemy lines, and they would have had a long walk ahead of them.

We picked up a British flight sergeant who had been shot down thirty days earlier. He had been living in the woods while gradually making his way west, hoping to meet our advancing forces. He immediately asked for a map, and then began detailing enemy forces, armor, artillery, and strength in each town through which he had passed. When he finished, the map was full of all the information he had given us. The Germans in those towns never knew what hit them. That man was fantastic in remembering every detail.

As we approached Warburg, a group of Military Government fellows joined us. We asked them what they were up to, and they advised that they had been ordered to secure a Leica camera factory in a town near Warburg. They knew exactly where they were headed, and they took that factory before it was destroyed or taken by us. We would have enjoyed having nice Leica cameras.

We entered Warburg and occupied that city — the easternmost position of the allied advance — for about a week. With a major section of the German army trapped between Warburg and the Rhine, we settled in. We listened to British Broadcasting stating that allied planes were searching the skies, but the Luftwaffe was nowhere to be found. That was odd, because every day we were in Warburg, we were strafed and bombed. We called for air support but didn't see an American plane for a week. One day, a German plane was strafing and bombing and he released his spare gas tank. I watched that tank as it seemed to hang in the air and then come down in a gentle arc until it struck the top of a three-story house about a block away. I couldn't take my eyes off it as it slowly moved through the air. The moment the tank hit the house, it was engulfed in flames.

While in Warburg, we received a message that a hundred German tanks were moving toward our positions. We kept asking for confirmation of the position of this column and its direction, but we never received any further information. Thankfully, the tanks never did appear.

On about the seventh day, a plane came right across the rooftops, and we opened fire immediately. Then it zoomed up, and we saw that it was an American P-51, but it was already hit. The pilot crash-landed just outside of Warburg and was picked up and brought in. Luckily, he landed in our area of control and only suffered a broken arm. He was furious that we had shot him down. He was able to stay with us a short time to enjoy the Luftwaffe attacks. I think he had a different point of view after he was evacuated.

One day while in Warburg, Corporal Bransky and I were looking for weapons. We entered this duplex-style home and went into a second floor apartment. There were eight Germans, six men and two women, sitting at a round table near the entrance. As soon as we entered I sensed

GERMANY EDITION
Wednesday, April 18, 1945
Volume 1, Number 14

THE STARS AND STRIPES

Daily Newspaper of U.S Armed Forces — in the European Theater of Operations

PASS IT UP FRONT!
Keep This 8 & 8 Moving.
Others Like It, Too!

Yanks Peril Leipzig, Chemnitz

Yanks Peril Leipzig and Chemnitz

(Continued on Page 4)

Combat Command A by-passed the city to reach Wurzenn, 12 miles to the east, while Combat Command B drove 5 miles east.

Associated Press front reports said that approximately 40,000 enemy troops in Leipzig had geared themselves for a "Stalingrad stand" in the city, where the population, which totalled a million before the war, showed signs of wanting to surrender.

A similar envelopment movement was beginning at Chemnitz. The 6th Armd. Div. of Lt. Gen. George S. Patton's U.S. 3d Army was driving 5 miles north of the industrial city while other forces were two miles away to the west.

Southward, the 90th Inf. Div. was within six miles of the Czech border.

On Lt. Gen. Alexander Patch's 7th Army front, troops of the 45th Inf. Div. were fighting in Nurnberg, entered Monday.

Except for isolated pockets, all northern Holland was cleared of Germans, and infantry of the Canadian 1st Army spread out along the North Sea coast. The Canadian 3rd Inf. Div. reached the North Sea northeast of Leeuwarden, and the 2nd Inf. Div. closed up on the coast north and northeast of captured Groeningen.

Shelled from Islands

Canadian forces in that sector were being shelled from the Frisian Islands, where 5,000 to 10,000 Germans were cut off from the mainland. Signs that these forces were starting to evacuate started to appear in reports of an attack by planes of the 2nd TAF on nine ships of a German convoy.

Enemy movement was also reported in the Zuider Zee as Germans acted to defend the municipal areas of western Holland by opening the Zuider Zee sluice gates and flooding coastal areas near Hilversum.

Front reports said that the German lines before Hamburg were beginning to crumble under thrusts of British 2nd Army tanks toward the Elbe River estuary. British armored columns advanced 22 miles in 24 hours, captured Schwerdingen, plunged five miles beyond and last night were still driving toward the Elbe.

It was disclosed yesterday that in the first 16 days of April, 755,573 prisoners have been taken by the Allies—almost half the estimated force opposing Gen. Eisenhower's offensive at the time of the Rhine crossing.

Of the total, 220,225 were captured by the 9th and 1st Armies in the Ruhr Pocket.

9th Battling Foe Inside Magdeburg

A cohesive Allied line was taking shape along the valleys of the Elbe, Mulde and Saale Rivers yesterday for the first time since the Rhine breakout as the American advance through Germany slowed down 45 miles from Berlin and 90 miles from the Russian lines.

U.S. troops, after advances of up to 200 miles in less than two weeks, have paused for a breather which will enable them to bring up supplies, strengthen communications and clean out enemy pockets left in the swift sweep into the Reich.

On Lt. Gen. William H. Simpson's 9th Army sector, tanks and infantry battled into Magdeburg in an all-out struggle to win the city after heavy air strikes. Leading elements were meeting stiffening resistance as they punched toward the Elbe, where the bridges were reported still intact.

Mop Up in Mountains

Tank, infantry and artillery units of the 83rd Inf. Div. counted 15 to 20 enemy tanks knocked out in the German counterattack Monday. To the south, other 9th Army elements were mopping up remnants of enemy units cut off in the Harz Mountains.

Little change was reported on Lt. Gen. Courtney Hodge's U.S. 1st Army front. The 9th Armd. Div. was enveloping Leipzig, Germany's fifth largest city. (division's)

(Continued on page 4)

---

something was wrong. Bransky spoke German, so he questioned them. They denied having any weapons. I kept thinking that if I was at home and enemy soldiers entered I would be up tight too and this justified my sense that something was wrong. I didn't know how to differentiate between fear and tension, but they certainly didn't show fear. We finally left but I was still not satisfied.

Some time later, too late to do anything about it, it suddenly hit me as to what was wrong. Those men were of military age and in excellent health, but were wearing civilian clothes. These many years later, I am convinced they were soldiers who had taken off their uniforms and were passing themselves off as civilians.

On Easter, a beautiful cloudless day, a German in civilian clothes handed me his luger pistol. It was practically new, as the pistol grips were not even stained. I still have that weapon today — along with a Nazi flag, Nazi armband, Nazi belt buckles, the map we used, medals, etc.

During this time, we heard rumors that we were to be ordered to take the city of Berlin. We all knew that the German army was crumbling, but there was still plenty of sting in it, and none of us thought that a surrender was imminent. We felt that the fanatics controlling the country would fight to the last foothill, and that we would have to ferret them out. It was not a pleasant thought, but I don't think that anyone disagreed with it at the time. After hearing that we were to take Berlin, we heard that the Russians objected to this, and our orders were changed.

Here's the way the booklet The 9th described our next phase:

"The 9th now assumed a spearheading role, leading the way for the First Army's drive eastward. The race through central Germany began April 10. Division tanks smashed so deeply into the enemy's rear that Nazis became hopelessly confused. Communications were slashed, vital supply points seized.

"In their April operations, the 9th's combat commands advanced approximately 280 miles — from Warburg to the Mulde River — in carrying out the encirclement of Leipzig. Attacking abreast, the three combat commands captured hundreds of cities, thousands of prisoners, knocked out scores of German tanks, guns, and vehicles."

As we were advancing toward Leipzig, we received a powerful signal from a radio station asking for our position in clear text. I radioed back, asking for identification, and received an unrecognizable code. I immediately reported the station and was told to keep in touch with him. Apparently range finders were placed on our transmissions, and I was told almost immediately to drop the station and change frequencies, as it was a power station near Leipzig. We had prearranged signals to our stations that would allow a rapid change of frequencies.

During this advance, I came down with a slight case of dysentery. Since we were constantly on the move, this necessitated use of the back door of the half-track to an extreme. My rear end hung out of that door until I finally shook off that illness. I am sure that the vehicles following were pleased to see the end of me — so to speak.

Again from The 9th:

Lieutenant Colonel Wesner and his driver, Corporal Sam Pernicci, East Point, Louisiana, captured a bridge intact over the Saale River near Naumburg. When they removed the charges from the bridge, the 9th's column rolled on without stopping.

"Rugged fighting developed through the thick defense belt around Leipzig. Germans used hundreds of ground-mounted antiaircraft guns, 500 of which were either knocked out or found abandoned by CCA.

"The same combat command captured a radio-radar station at Audgast, reputed to be the most powerful in Germany [probably the one that was trying to ascertain our position during the advance], as well as seizing an airfield at Polenz containing 250 planes.

German convoy comes in to surrender near Leipzig.

"The 2nd and 69th Infantry Divisions completed the capture of Leipzig, Germany's fifth largest city, after the 9th had completely encircled the area.

"The division's drive to the Mulde, in the military sense, split Germany in two. Instead of rolling eastward to link up with Soviet forces, the division was taken out of the lines for a well-deserved rest."

Before we reached Leipzig, we were near the small city of Bourne when I was working on the radio network and suddenly long dashes broke our transmission. (This is a standard interrupt signal.) We stopped and picked up in clear text: "We are being - - - - - - ." We called the station but received no response. There was no question what that message was, and we knew the general area of that crew. We were advised that a tank destroyer unit was in the area. They had been ambushed, and some were captured. They were taken into bunkers on the outskirts of the city, but we had the city surrounded. All night long, our forces pounded the area. During the night, an SS officer and the Volkstrom major were arguing within earshot of our men. The SS guy wanted to kill the men and the major wanted to surrender. Finally, the SS officer left and the major came and asked our fellows to contact the Americans. They agreed to do it, but not until after daybreak. The amazing part of all this is that for the rest of the night, the Germans polished their boots, belts, and gear to prepare for an official

An army travels on its stomach: chow time.

dress surrender. The following morning, contact was made with the tank destroyer unit. The Germans marched out in formation, all spit and polish, and surrendered to a group of Americans in rugged combat dress.

In the ambush on our men, there was a short skirmish, after which the men abandoned the vehicle, trying to escape. One was killed and another had rolled into a ditch when a German fired at him at point-blank range, hitting him in the center of the helmet over his eyes. The bullet penetrated the helmet, turned and traveled the dome of the helmet, and then exploded through the rear. The helmet had a deep groove, made by the bullet, from the front hole to the rear. We knew that our buddy was seriously injured, but we never heard another word about him.

During the advance to Leipzig, we had surrounded a city, and two of our men were ordered to take a message to the other side of the city. This meant a long ride around, covering miles of roads that were cleared only to the edges. Columns usually were not attacked, but single vehicles would run into ambushes. The driver turned to his buddy and said, "Let's go right through the city." He agreed, and they unpacked a case of hand grenades and took off. They surprised the Germans by zipping right through the city. While the driver was steering, his buddy kept tossing hand grenades over his shoulder to distract the Germans on the streets.

After the fellows delivered the message to the other side of the city,

Believe this heading is a misprint as the second word should be arm'd

9th Army By-Passes Leipzig

By JAMES M. LONG

Paris, April 14 (*AP*).—Three tank columns of the U. S. 1st and 3rd armies drove deep beyond embattled Leipzig in the heart of Germany today and ripped through rear supply and communications bases of the German army on the Russian front, now 85 miles or less to the east.

(The American Broadcasting Station in Europe told the German people that the entry into Berlin was "imminent" and asserted a "state of tension" existed in the capital, now menaced by A m e r i c a n forces 45 miles away and Russian troops 30 miles away.

(The United Press quoted German reports as saying that the U. S. 9th Army 2d Armored Division was only 21 miles from Berlin 24 hours ago, while the Exchange Telegraph A g e n c y quoted Radio Luxembourg as saying, without any confirmation, that Allied tank spearheads were within 13 miles of the battered German capital.)

As American armored columns roared 10 miles or more eastward under a partial news blackout in the center of Germany, one infantry unit was only 18 miles from the Czech frontier.

The 1st's 9th Armored Division and the 3d, 4th and 6th Armored divisions had struck so deep into the enemy's rear that the Germans now must turn for a back-to-back death stand or be cut off from retreat into the southern mountains.

Already this mountain fortress of Bavaria and Austria had been penetrated on the north by yet another 3d Army column—the 11th Armored Division — which roared into the Wagnerian city of Bayreuth, 124 miles north of Munich and 173 miles from Hitler's retreat at Berchtesgaden.

The battle for refugee-packed Leipzig, 75 miles southwest of Berlin, thundered into its second day. The 9th Armored Division quit the Leipzig siege and joined the powerful eastward push.

North of Leipzig, the 1st Army's 3d Armored Division broke loose on a 30-mile gallop that reached a point three miles south of Dessau, six miles from the Elbe river, and 55 miles southwest of Berlin itself.

they had to get back. They looked at each other and shrugged. So, down through the city they went again, using the same technique. They returned without a scratch — in a tenth of the time it would have taken them otherwise. Oddly enough, it was also a much safer trip. It may sound crazy, but their chances of survival probably were ten times better doing what they did. Snipers along the cleared highway probably would have picked them off.

One night during the advance, the Germans jammed our radio transmissions with a vengeance. They zeroed in on our frequency and transmitted a German band playing music, Adolf Hitler giving a speech, and Morse code on top of our Morse code. But the worst part was a radio operator inserting dots and dashes into our transmissions. That night, we really earned our board and luxury accommodations.

Some Germans had taken refuge in a boggy area that was densely covered with bushes like small saplings, about one to two inches in diameter. We were there with a tank and about six men, and it looked like they would be forced to go into the thickets after the Germans because the tank could not maneuver in there. It did not look like a pleasant situation. In frustration, the gunner on the top of the tank fired his .50-caliber machine gun into the thickets. Suddenly the Germans were crying, "Comrade," and out they came. Those bullets from the machine gun must have sounded like a hundred guns as they broke off those thickets, snapping branches. We were delighted to accept the surrender of those men.

It was along here that the men were talking about the Buchenwald concentration camp. They were horrified by what they had seen. The graphic details of what was there were enough for most of us. I had the opportunity to go and see for myself, but I turned it down — there is such a thing as being a glutton for punishment. I do remember the strong smell around that area, and I have often wondered how the people who lived in the area could deny that they knew what was going on.

We were ordered to stop near the Mulde River and wait for the Russians to come to us. It seemed as though we were always subject to the whims of the Russians. But this gave us a bit of a break, and we were billeted in a small city. One of our fellows came and announced that he had found one of our buddies in a railroad car awaiting processing for burial. Three of us went to the car, where he was stretched out alone, still wearing his helmet and apparently awaiting other casualties to be picked up by the Graves Identification Unit. We paid our last respects to him there, not realizing that he would be our company's last casualty of the war.

According to The 9th:

"An additional assignment remained, however, before the Germans were thoroughly beaten. When the enemy threatened a prolonged fight in Czechoslovakia, the 9th was sent on a long march south to join Third Army and help administer the coup de grace.

"CCA advanced into Czechoslovakia with the 1st Infantry Division. By the time the combat command linked up with the Red troops near Karlsbad, the Germans were completely kaput.

Heading for Czechoslovakia from Lobstadt, Germany. Roads are clear of enemy to the shoulders or woods.

"Being in the fight until the closing moments was more than an ordinary triumph for the gallant men of the 9th Armored. The Germans had reported them completely destroyed on three separate occasions. Yet, despite bitter fighting, sometimes against heavy odds, the men of the 9th held without yielding until their mission — the destruction of the enemy — was accomplished.

"Germany surrendered unconditionally at Rheims, France, May 8, 1945, two months to the day from the time the 9th seized the Ludendorff railroad bridge at Remagen, which sped victory for the allied nations."

When we were ordered south from the Mulde River, we raced down the Reichsautobahn, the German superhighway, at great speed for a tank division. Since we were the only traffic on the Autobahn, it was a surprise to see a Jeep coming in the opposite direction. We were probably doing forty-five miles per hour, and the Jeep was easily doing that when it passed. We were surprised to see that the Jeep had four stars mounted on the front bumper, and we debated whether the general was General Hodges or General Patton. There really was no way of knowing.

We moved over the border into a small town in Czechoslovakia and were amazed at the size of the people. This small town had people just as small — about four feet six — and all of the buildings were built to their scale. I had to duck when I entered a doorway, and with my helmet

Eger, Czechoslavakia: destroyed airfield.

Elbogen, Czechoslovakia: 60th Armored Infantry Battalion cleaning their guns the day war ended — just in case it isn't true.

Weiden, Germany: Listening to Winston Churchill advise us of the German surrender, then to General Leonard.

removed, my hair touched the ceiling of the room. I am five feet seven inches tall, and it was a new experience for me to have to duck on entering a house.

We were to receive the last hostile enemy shelling of our positions in Czechoslovakia. These probably were among the last shells fired by the enemy in the war.

We suddenly received orders to dig in and hold our positions, and then we were ordered to Elbogen, Czechoslovakia. We thought this was really strange, because none of us even considered that the Germans might be surrendering. What we didn't know was that our own officers were negotiating the surrender with the German commanders.

Soon we were told that the Germans were surrendering and that we should withdraw to the city of Weiden, just over the border in Germany. At Weiden, we were ordered to gather around radio sets that could receive the BBC, which we did. Winston Churchill came on the air and advised us in a stilted British accent, "The Germans have surrendered, the war is over!" All of us who sat there listening received the news very quietly — and partly in disbelief. We later heard about all the wild celebrations in the States when this news arrived, but it was a very somber and quiet group there in Weiden.

Churchill's statement that the war was over was not true as far as we

Weiden, Germany, May 8, 1945: "The War Is Over in Europe." All of us listened to the speeches and wild victory celebrations. Left to right, bottom: Orcutt and Reiners; center, Koppelman and Beat; top, Waterman, Wilson, Griswold, and Knachel. In window: Bransky.

were concerned, because all of us were well aware that the war was still raging in the Pacific. The typical reaction at the time was that we all hoped we would get a trip back to the States before being sent to the Pacific. None of us doubted that we would be on our way into the Asian Theater of Operations.

We were then ordered back into Czechoslovakia to remove the surrendering Germans to prison camps. I had a small detail with me, and we were getting along famously. One group would count sixty-five prisoners and march them to a 6X6 truck. Then we would order them into the truck, saying that the last man in the truck would get shot. It didn't take long for the truck to be full, but as usual, at least one sad sack would make two or three valiant attempts to get into the truck, stumbling each time. Then two of us, one on each side, would take him by the collar and the seat of the pants and heave him up on top of the rest of the prisoners — a truck containing sixty-five prisoners is fairly well packed. Actually, the speed with which we removed prisoners from that area meant that they would quickly get to prison camps, where they would be fed two solid meals a day. We had no intention of shooting any of these prisoners, but of course we didn't tell them that.

Just as fast as sixty-five men could be segregated and loaded, we would have them on their way. Everything was moving along nicely until I heard an angry voice behind me say, "Sergeant, what do you think you are doing? You are breaking the Articles of War." I turned around, laughing, and asked him what the Articles of War were. I thought he was kidding, but he was a U.S. Army captain, and he soon let me know that he wasn't kidding. He demanded to see my commanding officer. I turned to him and asked, "You are ordering me to have my commanding officer come here?" He responded that he was, and I was delighted. I turned to one of the men and said, "Go get the colonel and tell him this captain demands that he come here." I thought to myself that this yoyo would really get leveled by the colonel.

When the colonel arrived, the captain identified himself as being a captain from the Military Government in command of all operations in that area. I was shocked. Here was a captain pulling rank on a colonel. The colonel wasn't foolish, though, because he immediately asked the captain, "You don't like the way that my men are acting, Captain?" The captain responded in the negative, and the colonel turned and called,

~~RESTRICTED~~

HEADQUARTERS
9TH ARMORED DIVISION
AFO 259, U. S. ARMY

GNWHG

GENERAL ORDERS)   9 May 1945.
                       :
NUMBER   81)

ED OF WAR WITH GERMANY

1. Today, May 9, 1945, at 0001B, the German forces surrendered unconditionally and hostilities in Europe ceased.

2. This surrender was signed May 7, two months to the day after the 9th
Armored Division electrified the Allied World by seizing the Ludendorf railroad
bridge at Remagen, and establishing the first Allied bridgehead over the Rhine.

3. Let all offer a humble prayer to Almighty God that He may have mercy
on the souls of our gallant comrades who have paid the supreme sacrifice in our
march to this glorious victory.

4. Upon us who have been privileged to carry on to this hour of triumph
and rejoicing, there remains the responsibility of continuing to give our best
to whatever duties lie ahead.

5. I need not go over your sacrifices, your deeds of valor, and your
accomplishments. You know them -- the Army knows them -- the world knows them.

6. I have had the privilege of belonging to the 9th Armored Division since
its activation July 15, 1942, and the honor of commanding it since September 25,
1942. No commander ever had more justification for pride in his command. I
deeply appreciate your achievements and I thank you with all the sincerity
I possess for the work you have done.

JOHN W. LEONARD,
Major General, U. S. Army,
Commanding.

DISTRIBUTION "A"

ATTACHED UNITS:
    509th CIC Detachment
    3600th QM Truck Co
    3458th QM Truck Co
    482d AAA AW Bn (SP)
    656th TD Bn

~~RESTRICTED~~

End of War with Germany, May 9, 1945.

"Load up, men, we are going home." We loaded up and left the area and the captain and all of his German prisoners. I still didn't know what that strange thing, the Articles of War, was all about. The enemy could shoot our men in cold blood and shoot us down under a white flag, but for some strange reason, I was violating these screwball Articles of War by ordering prisoners into a truck.

It was not long before each man in the division was given the following:

Headquarters
9th Armored Division
APO 259, U.S. Army
General Orders #81   9 May 1945
End of War with Germany

1. Today, May 9, 1945, at 0001B, the German forces surrendered unconditionally and hostilities in Europe ceased.

2. This surrender was signed May 7, two months to the day after the 9th Armored Division electrified the Allied World by seizing the Ludendorff railroad bridge at Remagen, and establishing the first Allied bridgehead over the Rhine.

3. Let all offer a humble prayer to Almighty God that He may have mercy on the souls of our gallant comrades who have paid the supreme sacrifice in our march to this glorious victory.

4. Upon us who have been privileged to carry on to this hour of triumph and rejoicing, there remains the responsibility of continuing to give our best to whatever duties lie ahead.

5. I need not go over your sacrifices, your deeds of valor, and your accomplishments. You know them — the army knows them — the world knows them.

6. I have had the privilege of belonging to the 9th Armored Division since its activation July 15, 1942, and the honor of commanding it since September 25, 1942. No commander ever had more justification for pride in his command. I deeply appreciate your achievements and I thank you with all the sincerity I possess for the work you have done.

John W. Leonard,
Major General, U.S. Army
Commanding

Attached Units:
  509th CIC Detachment

3600th QM Truck Co.
3458th QM Truck Co.
482nd AAA AW Bn. (SP)
656th TD Bn.

The war in Europe was over, but all of us knew that there was still the Asian Theater of Operations actively fighting the Japanese. We were awarded the Victory Medal, and our company also was awarded the Meritorious Service Award Plaque.

149th Armored Signal Company, Headquarters, Bayreuth, Germany.

Twelve

The Occupation of Germany

We were ordered to leave the Weiden area and move north to the city of Bayreuth. When we arrived there, we found they had chosen a very nice residential area just across from a pretty walled park for our company, which once again was united. All of the residents of the buildings facing the park were ordered to move into the residences that were across the backyard from them — in essence, they had to vacate their homes for our use. Our company moved into those homes, and the company mess was set up along the street. The commanding officer set up his office at the end of the street. This was to be our home for about four months.

We were not in Bayreuth very long before we received a direct order from General George S. Patton, relayed to our company from SHAEF (Supreme Headquarters, Allied Expeditionary Forces). The order traveled from Third Army Headquarters to SHAEF to First Army Headquarters to 9th Armored Division Headquarters to our company. The order was that every man in our company was to spend the next thirty days learning how to salute. It seems that the general we passed on the Reichsautobahn when we were heading for Czechoslovakia was George S. Patton, and nobody in our unit saluted him. Since we already had received orders not to salute during combat, the whole thing seemed ludicrous. But of course we all knew that the general's order had to be obeyed, because you do not challenge the order of a four-star general. In obeying his order, we followed army regulations, which in essence say that men may be excused to carry on the business of the company. All of us immediately applied for an excuse, insisting we had temporary duty elsewhere. The CO was sympathetic to our requests, and the only ones who ended up learning to salute for thirty days were the goof-offs whom the CO wanted to punish. (Not long afterward, General Patton died in an automobile accident.)

We were then advised that in order to have a victory celebration, three bottles of liquor would be issued to every two men. This was the craziest idea anyone ever thought of. Here we were, armed to the teeth, and then every man in the unit is given an overabundance of booze. It probably was one of the most dangerous periods of the war. Men who

Bayreuth: Our mess hall on the street, park on other side of wall.

were absolutely stoned were firing machine guns and rifles and whooping it up. Some of us were stone sober and did not enjoy the celebration in the least. It was a miracle that no one was injured. The German civilians did not appear on the streets for three days for fear of exciting a drunken soldier. Finally, the booze ran out and things returned to what could reasonably be called normal.

One thing became apparent almost immediately: Now that we were more involved with the local population, there wasn't a Nazi in Germany. The Nazi war machine had instigated a world war, yet there wasn't a Nazi to be found. The people all blamed the Nazis for their problems and their final defeat, but it seemed there was a phantom crew of Nazis who had done it all. I, for one, refused to swallow that line.

One morning, we heard a shot in the company area and immediately went to investigate. Unfortunately, one of our lieutenants, apparently depressed over the loss of some of his men during the campaign, took his own life. He was a good officer, well liked, and always in the thick of it. It was a shock to all of us.

We had strict orders not to fraternize with the Germans — which, of course, created major problems for the army. Here were a group of young American soldiers surrounded by German women, and the army told us we couldn't fraternize. It was also true that the German male population

The Park, Bayreuth, Germany.

Nazi shrine to unwed mothers.

had been greatly reduced during the war, and most of the eligible German males were either dead or in prisoner-of-war camps. So there was an abundance of women looking for companionship — in the midst of a lot of young men away from home. The army tried to enforce its nonfraternization policy, but to no avail. It was kind of humorous. Here was an order coming from SHAEF that we should not fraternize with the women, and the officers, who were supposed to see that the order was carried out, were ignoring it. I don't remember the order being rescinded, but I think it was allowed to die on the vine.

In our specific case, our company was billeted at the edge of a beautiful park, it was May, and the weather was beautiful. As the saying goes, in the spring a young man's fancy turns to love, and that's just what happened. The army was destined to be defeated in its efforts. While all this was going on, the inspector general arrived in our company area. Our company had not reported any cases of venereal disease, and they wanted to know why. When questioned, we would respond immediately that it was against orders to fraternize with the civilian population. It was rather comical that they had ordered us not to do something and then had to investigate to find out how we were avoiding the problem.

Massive cleanup in Bayreuth.

The army began to relax orders considerably, and we received orders that every man would carry a weapon — for his own protection. They specifically stated that the weapon could be a sidearm and not of army issue. Almost all of us had automatics and pistols that we had acquired, and it was a lot more convenient to wear a sidearm than to carry a carbine. Of course, any time we would be on official business, we would revert to our army-issue weapons. At the time, I had a 9mm luger, 9mm Mauser with a wooden stock holster, and a .765 Mauser.

There was a heavily damaged building in Bayreuth that had been dedicated to Germany's unwed mothers. These women had dedicated their bastard children to Adolph Hitler and the Third Reich. It was almost a shrine. In the building was a statue of a mother with her children. Some of these children had grown enough so that Hitler had inducted them into the 11th SS Hitler Jugend Division. These were the trained little killers of the Führer. I often wondered what became of these children, raised by the state to devote their lives to Adolph Hitler.

The top priority of the army at that time was to try to bring normality back to the cities and towns. This meant trying to fix the bombed-out water and sewage systems, repairing the railroads and bridges, and also giving a decent burial to those killed in bombed and collapsed buildings. The German prisoners of war were put to work

German prisoners of war cleaned this up.

Our job was to remove the bodies for health reasons.

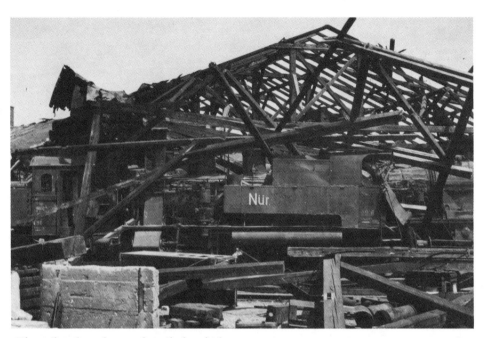

The railroad yards were heavily bombed.

repairing these parts of their cities. In Bayreuth, each morning, we would be taken to the prisoner-of-war compound, where we would pick up prisoners to escort to work details. Each American soldier would take 100 Volkstrom out for the day to work in areas that needed immediate repair. These prisoners had a hearty breakfast, worked all day, and returned to the compound, where they received a hearty dinner. This was far more than the German civilians were getting. The humorous part of this was that we would count 100 prisoners when we would leave the compound, and, after work, we would count the returning prisoners: 98, 99, 100, 101, 102. German soldiers hiding in the woods around the area would talk to the prisoners and find out that things weren't too bad, so they would join a group returning to the prison compound. This happened time and again. Of course, there was no way that one soldier could oversee a hundred prisoners, but the Volkstrom were not the problem soldiers of Germany, and apparently we didn't worry about whether we kept them all or not.

One group of prisoners for which I was responsible had to excavate a German barracks where about 300 soldiers had been caught by American bombers. (The city of Bayreuth had been bombed heavily near the end of the war.) In order to prevent epidemics, we had to dig down and remove these men for burial — not a pleasant task. We were all given inoculations to prevent disease.

Prisoners of war were put to work to get the railroads operating.

One day, I drew a group of SS, but these prisoners only went out in groups of five. The orders were that you took five, you brought back five. For some reason, they were short of guards that day, so they gave me ten SS to take to a stream that needed work. It was a shallow stream spanned by a small bridge with a low railing. I was barely two or three feet higher than the men. My orders were that nobody should approach them, that they would work all day, and that I would return them to the compound. Some women tried to bring them something in a container — probably food — and I ordered them away. These were SS, Hitler's elite, and they were to be treated as such. After a number of attempts by the women to pass them something, one of the SS men threw down his shovel and said, "Nichts zu essen, nicht arbeiten." I knew what that meant — no food, no work. The other nine men all stopped working and looked at me. I had no love of the SS, but I did know that I could not let this develop any further. I put my leg up on the cement railing of the bridge and rested my elbow on my knee as I took dead aim with my carbine, between the eyes, on the SS who had spoken up. No one said a word. The SS guy slowly bent down, never taking his eyes off me, retrieved his shovel, and started to work. The other nine immediately went back to work. I had no further trouble with that bunch, and I returned all ten to the compound. The women expressed themselves vociferously, and since I didn't understand the language, I presumed that they were complimenting me.

It was amazing how fast repairs could be made.

Memorial Day occurred not long after we had arrived in Bayreuth, and our entire company marched down into the park. In a lovely, quiet area, near the lake, we held a very private service to honor the memories of our buddies. As each name was tolled, a volley was fired. It was a day of remembrance. Apparently the Germans either had been told or sensed that this was no time for any of them to be around. It was a very private affair, and rightfully so. Even the ubiquitous German children were nowhere to be seen.

According to Phantom Nine, "The division made a final count of its casualties on June 4. A total of 739 men had been killed in action or had died from battle wounds. Another five died of injuries. The wounded totaled 3,337, and the missing and prisoners of war 617, for a casualty rate of about 45%. While the sum of these figures, 4,698, is probably accurate, it would have been more had those wounded and those who died of wounds among the 617 missing or prisoners been included."

We played either baseball or softball almost every day. We had an excellent ballfield, and it was great to get out and play in these games. The weather was getting very warm, and we would return to the house hot and sweaty. In the entryway of the house, we kept a barrel of nonalcoholic beer, which made a good soft drink. One particularly hot day, I returned from a game, downed two or three glasses of beer, and became dizzy. I

We played baseball at the Sports Palace, Nürnberg, Germany.

Adolph Hitler reviewed 100,000 troops here in this stadium.

*Our quarters across
from the park.*

couldn't figure out what was wrong with me until one of the fellows told me that the beer had just been changed from nonalcoholic content to 10 percent alcohol. I was as tight as a tick.

One German prisoner who was released to return home found his frau in the company of one of our men. Our guy shot and killed him. Naturally, the American was brought up on court-martial, which was a major topic of conversation in the company. In an immediate postwar climate, things are different than in everyday life. We had been taught to hate the Germans, and this hatred doesn't disappear just because somebody signs a peace treaty. There is right and wrong and then there is a large gray area. Any number of our men went to the trial and testified that this man had been struck in the head with a pitched ball while playing baseball. They had noticed that he had acted a little strangely thereafter, but they didn't think anything of it. When he shot the German, it proved that he was still not right, and he had been temporarily insane. He was acquitted of any wrongdoing. None of us disagreed with this decision.

On July 15, 1945, the 9th Armored Division celebrated its third anniversary, and we marched to a parade ground somewhere in Bayreuth. It was obvious to all of us that there was no place for a tank division in the China-Burma-India Theater of Operations. We all knew that the division would be dismantled or be taken by units, but would

Left to right: Bransky and Fulton. The German army would have been proud to have them.

Bud Knachel.

Jack Griswold hamming it up.

not remain a single division. The islands and the Asian sector were totally unsuited to our style of combat. At this ceremony, the men who had earned decorations were recognized and awarded their medals, and General Leonard addressed us (see Appendix).

The company commander soon found that when we moved into Bayreuth, he had to settle disputes among the German civilians. Naturally, since we moved the local residents into other people's homes, and doubled them up, there were problems. Suddenly they became our CO's problems. He found that he was spending as much time settling civilian disputes as he was commanding the company. It didn't take the German civilians long to learn that they could have him referee their problems. In essence, he became the unelected mayor of the community.

One day, a few of us took a Jeep and were driving around out in the country when we stopped at a farmhouse. A woman came out and said, "Have you come for the general's eggs?" We said yes. She brought out a whole batch of fresh eggs and gave them to us, and we gave her C-rations in exchange. She didn't want to take them, but we insisted. We figured that if the general ever found out who had taken his eggs, we didn't want him to be able to claim that we had stolen them. He never did find out, and we certainly enjoyed our fresh eggs.

The German people were keeping up with all of the negotiations regarding which country would administer what section of Germany. We were not concerned with this, but the people of Bayreuth were extremely concerned. Almost immediately, they found out that we would be

withdrawing and that the Russians would take over from us when we left. They pleaded with us to stay and not turn them over to the Russians. We had nothing to do with this and could do nothing for them, but they thought that somehow we could. I never did understand the Russians telling us not to take Berlin, to stop at the Mulde River and wait for them, and then taking over areas that we had taken.

The USO shows were plentiful at that time, and we did enjoy them. Naturally, entertainment was what we were most interested in, and we would take in all the shows when they came. Just before the Battle of the Bulge, Bob Hope put on a terrific show for us. He was, and still is, quite a character. The entertainers would come to us and ask us for the latest GI jokes, and we would oblige. They were great at blending in those jokes with their routines. It would bring down the house. At the time,

First group to head out for the Asian war zone.

Our company is gradually being broken up and being sent to the CBI.

chocolate was a real rarity as far as the German civilians were concerned, so it was a big item on the black market (we had plenty of it). In one of the USO plays that we saw, a beautiful actress was chasing an actor across the stage when he turned on her and said, "What do you want, a chocolate bar?" The audience roared, and we could see the actress asking other members of the cast what he had said.

Right after the Germans surrendered, each of us received a booklet that advised us what would happen next. We were all wondering when we would be sent to the Pacific Theater. It was not a question of whether — it was only when and how. The booklet described a four-point system:

1. Length of military service
2. Length of service overseas
3. Participation in combat
4. Number of dependent children

It was recognized that with Germany out of the war, there would be an excess of servicemen. According to the point system, men who were not critically needed would be discharged, so men would be mustered out individually.

On August 6, 1945, Hiroshima received the first atomic bomb ever used in combat. We were delighted that something had been found that would bring this war to an end. Not long after that, the A-bomb was dropped on Nagasaki. We were sick of war, but we had accepted the fact that we would be heading for the Asian Theater of Operations, and now all of that, thankfully, was changing. Finally, the Japanese would be brought to the bargaining table and the war would be shortened. That bomb saved hundreds of thousands of us from having to invade all of those islands.

The Japanese surrendered on August 15 — V-J day — and once again the news was greeted very quietly by our men. We now could start looking forward to the day when we would start home.

We were awarded the Occupation Medal with Germany bar.

One day, I was ordered to appear before the commanding officer. I couldn't imagine what he wanted, except perhaps some special detail. He advised me that the army was looking for men who would be willing to spend some more time in Germany, and if I would consider staying for an additional year, I would be promoted to second lieutenant. I thanked

the CO for considering me, but respectfully declined. I have no idea how many of us received that "offer you can't refuse." Ironically, I remained in Europe for another six months before I finally was sent home.

Soon men began to depart from the company area. A group was transferred to the 4th Armored Division at Landshut, Germany. I was in the next group to be transferred — part of the long and intricate process of repositioning the troops in order to ship them home.

THE MANCHESTER UNION.

NUMBER 83, NUMBER 124   THE UNION, MANCHESTER, N. H. THURSDAY MORNING, AUGUST 23, 1945   PRICE: FIVE CENTS

STAGE SET FOR JAP SURRENDER

Runaway Freight Car Rams Engine Near Claremont

Two Employes, Injured; Derailments at Tilton, Lowell Delay Trains

Special to The Union.

CLAREMONT JUNCTION, Aug. 22—Two employes of the Boston & Maine Railroad were injured slightly here Wednesday afternoon when a runaway freight car crashed into the locomotive of an empty passenger train outside Claremont Junction station.

Fireman Thomas Dooley of Concord injured his knee and Lester E. Hill of Claremont Junction, a railway mail clerk, was thrown to the floor of the mail car next to the engine and sustained cuts and lacerations. Both were treated by a local physician and their conditions were reportedly not serious.

Under investigation

Railroad officials said they were investigating the manner in which the freight car, loaded with pulpwood, got loose at Claremont, two miles from here, and apparently sped down the slight grade, plunged into the standing passenger train. Railroad employes were unable to relate a warning ahead to the crew of the train in time to prevent the crash.

Stopped 600 Feet

TILTON, Aug. 22—Traffic on the White Mountain division of the Boston & Maine Railroad was tied up for more than three hours tonight as two cars of a 50-car southbound freight left the rails in the freight yards on the Northfield side of the Winnipesaukee river. No one was injured.

De Gaulle Makes Good Start, Delights Crowd

Speaks Near-Perfect English As He Thanks U. S.

WASHINGTON, Aug. 22—(AP)—A tall, soldier-statesman wearing the Cross of Lorraine got off to an impressive start today in his mission of cementing friendly relations between France and the United States.

Gen. Charles de Gaulle, arriving for a three-day state visit with President Truman, stepped from a giant transport plane and delivered a greeting in near-perfect English which assured—and delighted—the large crowd on hand to greet him.

Voices Thanks

"The first thing I want to say is thank you," smiled the general, immaculate in a gray French army uniform.

In the welcoming crowd were scores of top French and American diplomatic, military and naval officials, but de Gaulle appeared to be talking over their heads to a group of American soldiers and civilians when he said,

"Without you, the American people, led by your great President, Roosevelt and Truman, there would be no future for Europe and Asia, but only intolerable servitude.

"There would have been no freedom for the world; there would have been no victory."

In the great task of organizing the world for peace, the United

(Continued on Page Three)

Many Ex-War Workers in No Hurry to Obtain New Jobs

More Than Million Already Released Because of Contract Terminations; Some Refuse to Work at Reduced Pay

BY THE ASSOCIATED PRESS

Plants and shipyards throughout the country continued to scale down their payrolls yesterday, but evidence appeared that many former war workers were in no great hurry to obtain jobs in private industry.

An Associated Press survey showed far more than 1,000,000 persons already released because of war contract terminations, and brought into focus these significant developments:

1. Reluctance on the part of some to accept jobs paying less than war plants.

2. While long lines formed at U. S. Employment Service and state unemployment compensation offices in some cities, others reported jobs waiting for applicants who did not appear immediately.

3. Many workers and employers took leave for the duration.

35 MPH Pace Urged by White

Warns No Leniency Will Be Shown in Driving Violations

CONCORD, Aug. 22—Motor Vehicle Commissioner Virgil D. White appealed today to all drivers in the state of New Hampshire to continue to operate at reduced speed even though the federal government has lifted the 35-mile speed limit.

Commissioner White pointed

Russian Troops Occupy Sakhalin and Port Arthur

Formal Surrender in China Due in Nankin; Puppet Emperor Held

BY RAY CRONIN

Associated Press War Editor

Forces of the conquering Allied nations, led by General MacArthur, their supreme commander, will land near Tokio next Tuesday, Japanese time, and the formal instrument of surrender will be signed three days later.

The general disclosed his occupation-surrender timetable at Manila today and simultaneously announced the instructions he sent to the Japanese government and Imperial headquarters.

Other Developments

These other developments were reported from Pacific-Asiatic zones:

Russian airborne troops landed in the Northern Kuriles.

The bypassed Japanese at Mili atoll, in the Marshalls, surrendered to an American navy captain.

Soviet parachute troops landed at Port Arthur.

The Russians interned the Japanese puppet emperor of Manchuria.

Formal surrender in China was to take place at Nankin.

Formal surrender at Singapore was scheduled for early September.

Hours after MacArthur had announced his plans the Japanese Domei agency reiterated its previous statement that the first Allied airborne troops would land at the Atsugi airdrome on Sunday, Tokio time. It estimated initial occupation forces at between 50,000 and 60,000.

Domei warned the landing forces will be in full combat array and urged the Nipponese to start early trouble. Domei declared "feelings of hate and uneasiness are matured" but recalled the words of the throne not to give way to resentment.

The extent of the landings from the air was indicated in an Associated Press dispatch from Shimonoseki. The greatest fleet of transport planes ever assembled jammed two square miles of an Okinawa airdrome. The Army Transport Command had concentrated airliners from all over the world to get all sorts of announced reunion. Undoubtedly these air giants will take part in the Atsugi landings Tuesday. Tokio newspapers continued to

(Continued on Page Five)

Wainwright M—

Be on Way Home

LITTLE NELL IN NEW SETTING—N. H. BOY IN CAST

"Little Nell," as enacted by members of a Seabee battalion at a Pacific base. The cast, left to right, Carl Older, SK 3/c, Chicago, Ill.; Thomas Jasperson, Y 3/c, Los Angeles, Cal.; Al Fitzgerer, Y 3/c, Mt. Vernon, O.; Edgar Reed, MM 2/c, Marlboro, N. H.; and Joseph Previte, SK 3/c, Barnesboro, Pa.

280,000 Victims of Atom Bombs

More Dying Daily From Burns, Other 'Uncanny Effects,' Says Tokio

BY THE ASSOCIATED PRESS

Atomic bombs dropped on Hiroshima and Nagasaki killed or injured 280,000 persons and more are dying daily from burns and other "uncanny effects," Tokio radio said yesterday.

Two hundred thousand more were left homeless, according to the broadcast, recorded by the Associated Press in New York.

"Even those who received minor burns looked quite healthy at first only to worsen after a few days from some unknown reason and frequently died," the broadcast explained.

The Hiroshima bomb, dropped August 6 struck in the heart of the city during a crowded working period, killing 60,000, injured 100,000 and left 200,000 homeless. The Nagasaki bomb dropped August 9 caused 130,000 casualties.

Bans on Home Deliveries and Holiday Trains Lifted

Service for Housewives Slated for Nov. 1; Home-Building Restrictions Also Due for Discard by End of September

WASHINGTON, Aug. 22—(AP)—Off comes the limit on home deliveries by grocer and butcher and department store. They can offer housewives full service after November 1.

And the railroads have permission to run seasonal trains on a two-way run again. This will be a boon on Labor Day (this is — if the railroads can find the cars.

The Office of Defense Transportation cleared the country's transportation system nearer its peacetime paths.

Other agencies opened up on the reconversion throttle by:

1. Lifting the ceiling on pay rates for white collar workers.

2. Relaxing lumber controls which helps pave the way for complete release of home and business construction by October 1.

Were Earlier Date

Other data proved out early this month for business reactivation. Spokesmen for seven major industrial associations recommended

Lifts Rules on Vacation Trains

ODT Okays Seasonal Runs by Lifting Order Issued in January

WASHINGTON, Aug. 22—(AP)—The ban against operating seasonal railroad passenger trains to resort and vacation areas, in effect since January 11, was removed today.

The Office of Defense Transportation also announced the elimination of a requirement that no passenger train could be operated if it was unless occupancy did not average 35 per cent of capacity.

Sign Aug. 31 on U. S. Battleship, MacArthur Says

USS Missouri Picked: Details of Arrival Officially Revealed

MANILA, Thursday, Aug. 23—(AP)—Japan's surrender will be signed aboard the battleship Missouri in Tokio bay August 31, General MacArthur announced today.

It was the first official word we had of the signing. The 45,000-ton battleship participated with Admiral Halsey's 3rd Fleet last month in bombarding Japan.

Precise Instructions

The supreme Allied commander of occupation forces also announced details of the precise instructions sent the Japanese for evacuating key areas, disarming ships and coastal defenses and providing direct assistance to the landing forces.

In his midnight announcement an correspondents, MacArthur said that members of the Japanese Imperial general staff had been alerted to be on hand from 8 a. m. "D" Day (8 p. m. Monday, U. S. Eastern War Time) to meet the Allied commander for immediate settlement of reoccupation problems.

MacArthur will accompany airborne forces which will land at Atsugi airdrome, 15 miles southwest of Tokio, in a vast convoy of transport planes covered by fighters and bombers. The exact landing time was not announced.

Simultaneously, landing craft such as have put thousands of fighting Americans ashore on many Pacific islands will land Marines and bluejackets at the famous Yokosuka naval base, on Tokio bay approximately 15 miles southeast of Atsugi.

MacArthur said the Allied occupation force later will utilize the naval base, which, while the enemy has always closely guarded.

(Domei, Japanese semi-official news agency, said in a Tokio broadcast the first occupation troops probably would number 50,000 or 60,000.

(The agency reiterated a previous claim that the first Allied airborne landings at Atsugi airdrome would be made Sunday, as announced in Tuesday's Japanese Imperial headquarters communique.

(Domei said that all local civil administrators in the occupation area would remain in charge, but the Nipponese in occupied hands, are remain cal...)

German barracks in Landshut, Germany.

Thirteen

The Trip Home

After we said our good-byes to our buddies, we were driven by 6X6 truck to Landshut, Germany, and located in a German army barracks in that city — which was relatively close to Munich.

We were housed in a permanent barracks building that had double bunks made of wood. Almost immediately, we had problems with bedbugs. We would get up in the middle of the night, chase down those damned things, kill them, and then put a swastika on the side of the bunk. One fellow had seven swastikas by the time a medic heard of our plight. The medic gave us an amazing liquid that took care of everything — we painted that substance on the wood and that was it, no more problem. One application killed all of the bugs. Before the war, in the hotel business, I had been well aware of the difficulties created by bedbugs. When we had them in the hotel, we would close a whole floor and gas it for twenty-four hours. I went after the medic to find out what this product was, and he told me it was DDT — a new product that was developed during the war but later banned as an environmental hazard. It sure did the job for us, though.

We had an excellent softball team, and we were willing to play any other team anywhere. One of the places we played was in Nürnberg, where Hitler had been fond of staging parades for a hundred thousand troops. The army took that parade area and turned it into baseball fields. There were three full-size baseball diamonds on those parade grounds — a great place to play ball.

Our softball team had two pitchers, both of whom were great. One day a team wanted to play us — but only if we did not use the pitcher who had faced them the previous time. We agreed, and we all met at the ballfield. One of the lieutenants accepted all the bets on the outcome of the game and placed them in his helmet. By the time the game started, the helmet contained more than $5,000! One of our fellows remarked to the lieutenant that we expected to still see him when the game was over. We managed to shock that opposing team by having a better pitcher than we had had the previous time. As soon as the game ended, we collected from the lieutenant.

We had some fellows from Brooklyn who were rooters for the team,

Left to right: Stine, Dykehouse, Beach, McWhirter, and Herwig at the Schoch caserne waiting for trucks to transfer us to Vilshofen.

and I think they won more games for us than we won as players. They were experts at riling up the other players. I'll never forget the officer who was playing for the other team and tried to pull rank. (When an officer plays sports, he does not have the privilege of rank.) I almost felt sorry for him after a while. Every time he would come to bat, the cheering section would be called to attention to give him the respect he demanded. They would all jump to their feet and salute him at every turn. He was the happiest man alive to see that game end.

I was called to a dentist's office for a checkup, and he found that I had a cavity between my two front teeth. I don't know what kind of a dentist he was, but he sure did me no favor. He cemented the two front teeth together, and I had to have it all taken out after I was discharged. I have always feared that socialized medicine would keep someone like that incompetent dentist in business.

We played ball constantly in our free time and guarded prisoners during work details the rest of the time. I am not sure which we did the most, but I do remember the sports more than the other. One night, I had difficulty sleeping because of pains in my lower abdomen. After a few nights of this, I went to the medic, who asked me if I had ever had appendicitis. I told him no, and he immediately remarked that I had it now. Then I was sent to a doctor, who asked me what was wrong. I told

Army barracks at Pilsen, Czechoslovakia.

him that the medic thought I had appendicitis. As he began to examine me, I could see that he was puzzled. Finally, he looked at me and said, "Does your left leg below the knee feel as if it isn't there?" I remarked that I had not mentioned the leg, but yes, that was exactly the way it felt. It seems that I had torn a tendon from my hip to the crotch and down to just above the knee. He said it would take about six months to heal, and he told me to ease off on the sports for a while. Luckily enough, the summer season was practically over anyway, but that tendon never did fully heal. I still have that problem today.

In the strange ways and methods of the army, I was now transferred to the 83rd Infantry Division, supposedly to be processed home. Since this was farther east, I did not understand how this would speed up my trip home. I was only with the 83rd a short time, but there we were billeted adjacent to a soccer field, so we played football during the fall.

One night, I was assigned to guard duty and was standing at my position when I began to feel pressure against my right leg. It was pitch black, and a huge mastiff had quietly walked up beside me and then leaned against me. I almost jumped out of my boots. But he was a friendly cuss and stayed with me for the remainder of my shift. Apparently he was lonesome, and I was the only one up and around.

It didn't take the army long to transfer me again, and this time I

Skoda munitions factory in Pilsen.

Main street of Pilsen.

Statue of Masaryk, great Czech statesman. This is also where General Harmon stood to make his speeches.

couldn't believe it. I was transferred to the 80th Infantry Division and almost immediately was transferred yet again. I received orders to be transported to XXII Corps in Pilsen, Czechoslovakia. Every transfer so far had sent me farther east, and I just couldn't fathom how or when I would eventually start heading west toward home.

We arrived in Pilsen at a permanent army barracks, and I was assigned to take shifts on the army telephone switchboard. This was the busiest switchboard I had ever operated. There were eight switchboards, and an operator sat at each board. There are thirteen cords on a switchboard, and we would connect twelve of the cords and use the thirteenth to advise the callers that all lines were busy. There was one red light on the board, and all the rest were orange. We were advised that if the red light came on, we were to answer that light immediately. It was the commanding general of 22nd Corps. These army switchboards had a direct link into the civilian exchange in Pilsen. We would always have more orange lights lighted up on the board than we had cords to complete the calls.

As may be imagined, some callers became extremely frustrated when they could not place a call. One day, I plugged into one of the lines and started to tell the caller that the lines were busy, but he blasted away and demanded to be connected. I do remember making some remark to the

McAvoy just after being issued the new Eisenhower jacket.

effect that he could wait his turn, probably till hell froze over. The next thing I knew, armed MPs were all over the switchboard room. When I asked what was going on, one of the fellows told me that someone had told off the general. It seems that the general had left his office where the red telephone was and tried to place a call on one of the other telephones. Needless to say, the general was advised that this was a busy exchange and he did get preference, but only from his own telephone. We weren't mind-readers and did not have television as yet. Fortunately, that crisis blew over gently.

Pilsen was a black-market paradise. I didn't smoke, but cigarettes cost only five cents a pack. I found out I could exchange one pack of cigarettes for a fifth of brandy — that seemed pretty reasonable to me. The same fellow asked me what I would give him for a Leica camera. After dickering back and forth, we had arrived at a carton of cigarettes when he backed out of the deal.

The army, concerned about the black market, cut off all shipments of money home. This suddenly increased the pots in the poker games, as now there was plenty of money that had to be spent before returning home. Anything American could be sold for a fortune — especially food, chocolate, and cigarettes.

We were assigned to a young master sergeant who had just arrived

Stine in door on left in our 40-and-8 transportation to LeHavre.

from the States, and he was extremely embarrassed to have us under him. I have to admit that he used the right approach in asking for our cooperation while there. We did work with him and didn't cause him any trouble.

The downtown part of Pilsen was interesting, but the people were not very cordial. However, we did tour the city and enjoyed the sights while we were there, although it was winter, and we were limited in how much we could move about.

One day in early December, we received orders to depart by 40-and-8s to Camp Lucky Strike, LeHavre, France. We were delighted, but it was about the most uncomfortable trip we had in the army. The 40-and-8s were little railroad boxcars that were about one-third the size of our boxcars. They were designed to hold forty men or eight horses — hence their name. Meals were prepared in one of the boxcars, and the train would stop along the way so we could have meals and relieve ourselves. Washing and cleaning-up were almost no-nos. Not only that, but this was December, and there was no heat in the boxcars.

Our triumphal trip across France to enter combat was starkly different from our boxcar trip across France to go home. There were no cheering crowds, and almost the only people we saw were the troops moving up to replace us. We would look at these barefaced kids and

Our first-class train from Pilsen to LeHavre.

Camp Lucky Strike, LeHavre, France.

remark that they must be robbing the cradle to send them to take our place. It was humorous, in a way, because these fellows were only a year or two younger than we, but there was a strange difference that I never could quite explain. I know that experience was one thing, but it was more than that. We just looked older.

Finally we arrived at Camp Lucky Strike, where we were assigned tents and a place to sleep. We immediately headed for the hot showers and clean clothes. Next, we had to go through the process of sorting out what we were planning to take home with us and what we could take home with us. I was issued a license for my luger pistol as captured enemy equipment, and then I got licenses for sundry other captured enemy items: a German flag, shotgun, armband, belt buckles, bayonets, and even German medals. The luger and the shotgun were the only guns for which they would issue me licenses. I gave away my other guns.

The next order was to turn in all of our "invasion money." I had accumulated British pounds, French francs, and German marks, as well as money from Belgium and Czechoslovakia. It had never bothered me to carry this paper in my pocket, because it didn't seem like real money. I

Camp Lucky Strike.

CERTI.ICATE

5 December 1945
(Date)

1.   I certify that I have personally examined the items of captured enemy equipment in the possession of Sec A George E. Mc Avoy 11122455 and that the bearer is officially authorized by the Theater Commander, under the provisions of Sec VI, Cir 155, WD, 28 May 1945, to retain as his personal property the articles listed in Par 3, below.

2.   I further certify that if such items are to be mailed to the US, they do not include any items prohibited by Sec VI, Cir 155, WD, 28 May 1945.

3.   The items referred to are : 1 Pistol, Lugar, 9mm, Model 1938 Ser. No. 5318 W/holster & 2 Magazines ;

DORAN A. SAUERS   (Signature)

Capt.   (Rank, Branch and Organization)
CO. "G" 56th Signal Battalion

(This certificate will be prepared in duplicate)

AG USFET Form N° 33

Lof. 8-46 5.000.000 78.920

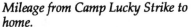

Mileage from Camp Lucky Strike to home.

Up the gangplank for our trip home.

arrived at the paymaster and laid out what I had. When he started to count out the equivalent in U.S. cash, I was stunned. He counted out $600 — the amount I paid for a new 1946 Chevrolet after I was discharged. It was far too much money to be carrying around, but I had never realized it.

We were at Camp Lucky Strike when I celebrated my fourth Christmas in the army — this time a very gay and devout holiday. We went to church and then gathered in the community building, where anyone who had an instrument became part of a makeshift orchestra. We sang Christmas carols and enjoyed the music. During the program, there was a little farmer-type fellow sitting with a banjo, and the orchestra leader kept featuring all of the other instruments but ignoring the banjo. Finally, almost in a condescending way, the conductor recognized the banjo player. I have never heard a banjo played like that before or since. That fellow stood that building on its ear and had the whole crowd with him from then on. I thought he was fantastic — and I am not a great fan of banjos.

While at Camp Lucky Strike, we were entertained and created our own entertainment, but we didn't stay long. We were advised that we would be sailing on the *USS Mount Vernon*, an army troopship, two days

USS Mount Vernon. We were single-file on the pier. Note the debris in the water.

It was cold and damp. Note the life rafts strapped to the deck.

*McWhirter hanging on.
Some of us were together
for three years.*

after Christmas. I had never realized that the army had a navy, but the *Mount Vernon* was operated by the U.S. Army and carried 6,000 troops.

We loaded on the ship the day after Christmas. As we marched down onto the dock, we could easily see the devastation wrought by the bombings by both sides. Obviously, they had cleared this pier in order to allow the ship to dock there. We had a little dachshund with us, and we were told that the dog could not go. We refused to accept that, because the dog belonged to us, and he was going with us. So we put him in a duffel bag and carried him up the gangplank and onto the ship.

This ship was designed just to carry troops, and every nook and cranny was put to use. There were large, dormitory-style sleeping areas with bunks, and centrally located showers and baths. The dining room had high-level tables so we could stand and eat. There were no chairs or lounge chairs anywhere.

After we were settled in, an MP caught our dog and put him off the ship. We were furious. That night, a guard was walking the dock, and we saw our dog down there with him. We called down and asked him if he would help us get the dog back onto the ship. He had real misgivings about doing it, but finally he agreed. We went around acquiring everybody's tent ropes and tied them together. Then we jury-rigged a basket at the end of the rope. We tossed the knotted rope down onto the

Huddled behind the superstructure, out of the wind.

pier and the guard put the dog into it. We then realized that we couldn't just swing him back to the ship, because he would crash into the side of the hull. He would have to go into the water first. So we told the guard to drop him into the frigid water, which he did. We towed the dog over to the ship and then lifted him up the side. The poor creature had pneumonia after that, but he survived, and we made sure that no MP would see him this time. That little guy was the best-guarded body on that ship.

Since the army had cut off all shipments of money home in order to stop the black market, the barbers had stopped cutting hair. This created a bit of a problem, as all of us were pretty shaggy, with hair over our ears. As soon as we got on the ship, we found out there was a barbershop aboard, and we all made for it. The barbers only used clippers and just sheared off the extra mop we were wearing. It wasn't a haircut — it was a shearing — but it was a pleasure to get rid of all that hair.

We sailed out of LeHavre directly into a severe storm. That was rough, but not nearly as bad as two days later, when we hit a really bad storm. There was a map on the wall, and a line would be drawn showing the progress of the ship each day. We would make about an inch and a half in twenty-four hours on that map, and the third day we made no progress at all. The sea was wild, and there were whitecaps on every wave. Oddly enough, I was seasick the first day out, but by the third day, it did not

The sea beginning to come over the prow the day after the severe storm.

affect me. When I went to the mess hall for dinner, the place was practically vacant — there wasn't even one man per table. Attempting to eat was a real adventure. I had my mess kit with my cup, knife, fork, and spoon, plus the kit cover and the bottom. When that was filled with food, I tried to lay over the table and surround the food, because the ship was rolling so much. It took some real planning to eat that meal. Obviously, about 5,500 of the men on board were not interested in eating.

The next day was partly sunny, but the sea was still violent. I decided to try to get a photograph of the ship as it rose above the waves and then plunged down into the sea. I wanted to get a shot of the sea coming up over the prow. Another fellow and I went up on the promenade deck and partially removed one of the wooden frames. We peeked out to see how the ship was doing, and when it began the plunge, I poked the camera out and took the picture. The second I shot the picture, we were doused with water from that small opening. We quickly closed it up.

At the same time, two men went down onto the stern of the ship. A wave came over, picked them up, and washed them right down the deck to the opening. They were too large to go through the opening, which was the only thing that saved them from going overboard. After that, the stern deck was posted off limits until the sea calmed.

That night, we celebrated — if you can call it that — New Year's Eve

The stern of the USS Mount Vernon. Two men were almost washed overboard from here.

twice as we passed the time zones near Newfoundland. This trip, the ship was not blacked out, so at least we were able to enjoy a little more air from the portholes than we had had on the *Queen Mary*. We were all pumped up about seeing the States for the first time in more than a year and finally arriving home. All during this time, the MPs on board ship had been throwing their weight around, issuing everyone orders and generally causing resentment. They were not being diplomatic, and most of the men on that ship no longer considered themselves part of the military. We were going home to a civilian life.

When we boarded the ship, we had been given orders to stay off the rigging. We all accepted that as a matter of course, but none of us had ever before felt the emotion of sailing into New York Harbor and seeing the Statue of Liberty and the New York skyline. Every one of the 6,000 men on that ship was vying for a position to savor that wonderful sight. It is something that cannot be explained — only experienced. The mental attitude of all of us on that ship was basically that there had been a call to war and we had responded. The war was now over, and in essence we were now civilians. It didn't make any difference that we were still in uniform — that was only because they had not been able to get us home as yet. The rigid discipline of the military was a thing of the past. I think that best sums up the mental attitude at that moment.

What a sight! The Statue of Liberty. We had orders to stay off the rigging and lifeboats.
At the first sight of her, there was no stopping anyone. You live for moments like this.

When land was sighted, there was a great stir. I was surprised that we would see land for so long a period before arriving in New York. I don't know how many hours we were within sight of land, but it seemed like a long time. Then, suddenly, there she was — the Statue of Liberty. The men leaped to their feet, jumped into the lifeboats hanging over the side, climbed the masts, climbed onto the life rafts — and generally grabbed any vantage point that would provide a good look at that grand old girl. Just imagine 6,000 men hanging from every pillar and post on that ship.

One of the MPs grabbed one fellow's ankle and yanked him off one of the masts. The fellow fell to the deck but landed on all fours, and he responded by throwing a punch from the deck that absolutely flattened the MP. Suddenly, a very ugly situation was developing right in New York Harbor — just when all of us were looking forward to getting home. A detachment of MPs arrived on the deck with the officer of the day, who started to place this fellow under arrest for slugging the MP. Another one of our guys stepped up to the officer and said, "Lieutenant, you are not taking this man anywhere." The lieutenant insisted that the offending fellow was being placed under arrest, but then he was told, "Lieutenant,

Home — after almost a year and a half overseas.

you have two choices: Either you and your MPs leave this deck or you all go over the side!" I take my hat off to that lieutenant, because he had brains enough to recognize a very dangerous situation. He ordered the MPs to leave the deck, ordered the men to break it up, and then he left. I figured that he was pretty smart for having defused an explosive situation that could have cost him his life. These men were not bluffing.

Next thing we knew, however, the MPs appeared at the top of each stairway to the next deck in full battle dress and fully armed. I guess the lieutenant decided that he would try to intimidate the men with a show of force. Instead, this infuriated everyone. For the rest of the way into the harbor, the men stood at the bottom of the staircase, taunting and daring the MPs to come down onto our deck and telling them what would happen if they did. At the time, I thought about how stupidly the whole incident had been handled. The overbearance of the MPs throughout the trip, the MP yanking a man to the deck and then getting knocked out by him, the lieutenant seeming to show common sense in defusing the situation and then lighting a fire under everyone by trying to intimidate the men with armed MPs. It probably was a good thing that the lieutenant was only in charge of a detail of MPs on a troopship instead of in the line, where his decisions may have hurt. The ship docked in New York without further incident, and no action was taken against any of the men.

A little ship tooted a greeting to us.

Only one little ship came out to greet us. It blew its horn, circled around, and left. I have always found it rather odd that our biggest victory celebration was that triumphal march across France — before we had even seen action. When we docked in New York, twenty-nine dogs marched down the gangplank off the ship, and one of them was a German shepherd. I don't know how they managed to smuggle that large a dog aboard the ship, because he would have taken up a whole duffel bag!

We went by ferry across the Hudson River and then back to Camp Kilmer, where we arrived at 2 a.m. We were taken immediately to the mess hall, where we were served sirloin steaks — as many as we wanted to eat. From Camp Kilmer, we were split up to leave for our different areas of residence, and I was ordered to Fort Devens, Massachusetts.

At Fort Devens, I was given a physical and put through the paper routine. Finally, I was issued my lame duck (honorable discharge) pin, my discharge, my mustering-out pay, and my train ticket home. On January 9, 1946, I boarded the passenger train from Ayer, Massachusetts, to Lewiston, Maine. When the train arrived at the railroad station in Portland, I was staring out the window, watching returning servicemen being greeted by their wives and families, when tears began to run down my cheeks. After three years, one month, and nine days, I kept repeating, "It's over, it's all over!"

Saturday, December 9, 1967: RMS Queen Mary was officially presented to the city of Long Beach, California.

R.M.S.QUEENMARY

Constructed by: John Brown & Co., Ltd., Clydebank, Scotland
Commissioned by: Cunard Steamship Co., Ltd.
Keel Laid: December 1, 1930
Date Launched: September 26, 1934
Maiden Voyage: May 27, 1936
War Service: March, 1940-September 1946
War History: Carried a total of 765,429 military personnel. Sailed a total of 569,429 miles (916,407km). Carried up to 15,000 troops at one time. Carried wounded returning to United States. Transported Winston Churchill three times to conferences. Carried 12,886 G.I. Brides and children.
Resumed Peacetime Passenger Service: July 31, 1947
Retired from Regular Passenger Service: September 19, 1967 (after completing 1,001 crossings of the Atlantic)
Departed on "Last Great Cruise": 9:30 A.M. Tuesday, October 31, 1967

Arrived at Long Beach, California: 10:00 A.M. Saturday, December 9, 1967
Change of Ownership: Removed from British registry and officially turned over to ownership of City of Long Beach at 10:00 A.M., Monday, December 11, 1967
Portholes: Over 2,000
Rivets: Over 10,000,000
Hull Plates: 8 ft. (2.44 m.) to 30 ft. (9.14 m.) in length; up to 1.25 in. (3.2 cm.) thick
Gross Tonnage: 81,237 gross tons (230,039 cu. m.)
Overall Length: 1,019.5 ft. (310.74 m.)
Moulded Breadth: 118 ft. (35.97 m.)
Height from Keel to
　Promenade Deck: 92.5 ft. (28.19 m.)
　Forward Smokestack: 181 ft. (55.17 m.)
　Top of Foremast: 237 ft. (72.24 m.)
Draft: 39 ft. 4-9/16 in. (12.00 m.)
Number of Decks: 12
Passenger Capacity: 1,957
Officers and Crew: 1,174

Length of Promenade Deck: 724 ft. (220.68 m.)
Cruising Speed: 28.5 knots (55.17 km./hr.)
Fuel Consumption: 13 ft./gal. (1 m./l.)
Rudder: 140 tons
Bow Anchors: 2 @ 16 tons (16,291 kg.)
Anchor Height: 18 ft. (5.48 m.)
Length of Anchor Chain: 900 ft. (274.32 m.)
Weight of Anchor Chain: 45 tons (45.818 kg.)
Anchor Chain Link: 2 ft. (61 cm.) long, weighing 224 lb. (101.8 kg.)
Whistles: 3 — Steam type. Two on forward funnel, one on middle funnel. Each over 6 ft. (1.83 m.) long, weighing 2,205 lb. (1,002 kg.)
Lifeboats: 24, powered by 18 H.P. (76.11 kg.-m per sec.) diesel engines
Lifeboat Capacity: 145 persons
Smokestacks: 3 — Elliptical in shape; 36 ft. (10.97 m.) fore and aft, 23.3 ft. (7.1 m.) wide
Height: Forward: 70.5 ft. (21.49 m.)
　　　　Middle: 67.5 ft. (20.57 m.)
　　　　Aft: 62.25 ft. (18.97 m.)

Appendix A

The following material is excerpted from R.M.S. Queen Mary, 50 Years of Splendour, *by David F. Hutchings.*

The ship that bore her name was not forgotten by HRH Queen Mary during the war. They exchanged messages many times. Her Majesty sent the following one just before D-Day:

"Since I launched the *Queen Mary* nearly ten years ago, almost half of her life has been spent on active war service. Now, as the war enters on this decisive phase, I send my warm greetings to the Captain, Officers and the Ship's Company, and to all those who sail in the ship that bears my name.

"It is always a source of pride and pleasure to me to receive news of the magnificent work the *Queen Mary* is doing in the transport of troops from every quarter of the Empire and Commonwealth, and from the United States of America, to the theatres of war. I pray that before very long it may be her joyful duty to carry the victorious soldiers of the United Nations back to their homes and families in many parts of the world.

"My earnest hope is that the many friendships born on board the *Queen Mary* during the years of war will continue into the happier years of peace to come, and that she will always prove herself a strong link, and a messenger of goodwill between the great English-speaking nations."

One particular celebrity who traveled on board the liner during the war was a gentleman who had the pseudonym of "Colonel Warden". Three times he traveled on the *Mary*, partly because of being affected by tuberculosis at one time, which prevented him from using aircraft. He always traveled with a large retinue and used the chance of sailing in the Cunarder to make several important decisions. The Mary would wait for him (one time for eighteen days) to rejoin her and he was always appreciative of her crew and qualities, and cabins were especially refurbished for his use. The man in question was Winston Churchill.

On April 4, 1945, the *Mary* arrived in New York where she was laid up for several weeks and drydocked. It was then decided that she would no longer be needed to transport American soldiers to Europe.

After the German surrender in May, VE (Victory in Europe) Day was celebrated in the United States, as elsewhere, and by this time both the *Mary* and *Elizabeth* were in New York. They joined in the ports armistice

Hotel Queen Mary,
Long Beach.

celebrations by adding to the crescendo of sound with their beautiful sirens.

To the American soldiers, the two queens, the *Queen Mary* and her sister ship the *Queen Elizabeth*, were so huge that they believed that only the United States could have built them.

The *Mary* made several more trips to Gourock but the number of eastbound passengers was low. Westbound, the numbers reflected the huge numbers of troops previously carried, but this time they were going home. With 14,777 G.I.s on board, the liner had a tremendous reception in New York with aircraft, boats, bands, and crowds cheering her in. It was, at the time, the largest contingent of soldiers to enter the port on one ship, just as she had carried the largest number of troops to depart, and the Mary had also had the honor of taking the first U.S. units home.

During the war years, the *Mary* had carried 810,730 passengers and steamed 661,771 miles. Winston Churchill felt that the queens' contribution to the war effort had shortened the conflict by a year. In his tribute to both queens, he said:

"Built for the arts of peace and to link the Old World with the New, the queens have challenged the fury of Hitlerism in the Battle of the Atlantic. At a speed never before realized in war they carried over a

The Queen Mary's first voyage to the United States after VE Day.

million men to defend the liberties of civilisation. Often, whole divisions at a time were moved by each ship....To the men who contributed to the success of our operations in the years of peril. . . . the world owes a debt that it will not be easy to measure."

On Saturday, August 11, 1945, zigzagging and blackouts ceased and the *Queen Mary* made her first postwar return to Southampton, again watched by thousands, berthing at 2 p.m., she was accompanied by airplanes and boats, with the Southampton Police Band and civic dignitaries welcoming her back.

She continued to repatriate American troops and the "GI Brides" - British girls who had married American servicemen and also girls who had married Canadians (the latter's wives were taken to Halifax, Nova Scotia). In all, the *Queen Mary* carried 30 percent of all the service wives, numbering 9,118 women and 3,768 children. During a drydocking, special facilities had been installed on board, and efforts had been made to try and return the *Mary* to some sort of prewar standard. The funnels had been painted in the cheery Cunard White Star colors and the standee bunks, armor, etc., had been removed.

On her return to Southampton on September 29, 1946, the *Mary* was finally demobilized to begin a ten month restoration back to her former

Hotel Queen Mary and the Spruce Goose.

luxury-liner status. All of the furniture and accessories had to be brought from storage from New Forest, Australia, and New York, where they had been sent ashore in the early part of the war for safekeeping. These had to be renovated and collated which was done at Fords, in huge sheds at Eastleigh near Southampton. A new stem was fitted, degaussing strips and their protective steel shielding were removed from around the sheerline, murals were renovated, and a thousand other tasks had to be completed to get the ship ready for sea. Men came from the Clyde to work on the liner, and 120 female French polishers were employed.

The *Queen Elizabeth* having been previously refurbished, was a model for renovating the *Queen Mary*. The *Queen Mary* had two garden lounges built on either side of the First Class smoke room, a permanent cinema was converted from the starboard gallery on the Promenade Deck, a cocktail bar now greeted passengers in the entrance to the main restaurant, and the gymnasium was moved to amidship on the Sun Deck. None of these amenities were available to the troops. Tourist Class now had its own self-contained section of the Sports Deck between the first and second funnels, and the crew had new accommodations. To aid in the navigation of the ship, "Seascan" radar was also fitted.

John Brown, her builders, reconditioned the *Queen Mary*, as the main contractor, and J. Thornycroft of Southampton was the main

Hotel Queen Mary and the Spruce Goose lighted at night.

subcontractor. Fifteen hundred men from Clydeside camped at Chandlers Ford and were taken each day to the liner. When the *Mary* was drydocked, her propellers were removed, her shafts were drawn out for inspection and her underwater hull was scaled and coated with 3,000 gallons of antifouling paint.

The *Elizabeth*, newly refitted, pristinely painted, and ready for her own, long-delayed commercial maiden voyage, passed the *Mary* when she returned to Southampton for her refurbishing.

On the very eve of the *Queen Elizabeths* maiden voyage, which took place on October 16, Sir Percy Bates died. He was thus denied the chance of seeing the realization of the concept that he had supported and fought for so long ago - the two-ship, weekly express service across the Atlantic.

The *Mary* was ready, by mid-July, to reestablish herself on her intended route, and she was well booked for her postwar debut. The week before she sailed for New York, she combined a trials trip to test her services with a short cruise, so on Thursday July 25, she left Southampton with 500 guests on board.

She returned the next day but anchored in Cowes Roads while the *Queen Elizabeth* sailed by, the two mammoth liners exchanging greetings. The *Mary* then entered Southampton Docks, occupying the berth recently vacated by her newer sister.

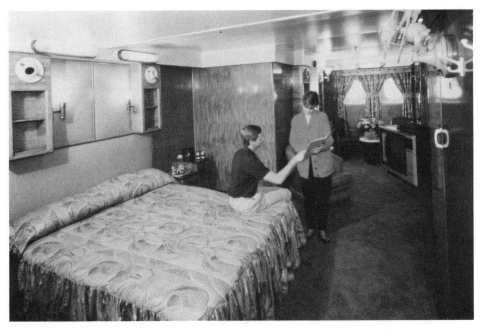

The luxurious accommodations available today, Hotel Queen Mary.

She sailed for New York on the following Thursday with 2,000 passengers. The queens had at last laid claim to their rightful domain and together they would rule for the next eleven years.

The *Queen Mary* carried stars and made stars. She, herself, became a star of films and television shows, proving that once "on stage", she could not be "up-staged". Frank Sinatra costarred with the liner in Assault on a Queen, made in 1965, when she played herself. Luckily, it was the only time in her career when a U-boat got the better of her! She took on a part in the Poseidon Adventure, the first and best of a spate of pseudo-disaster movies, that was based on Paul Gallicos book. In this she played the fatally unstable SS *Poseidon*, although mainly in model form. Parts in various "soap" television detective series followed, but she had taken to her recent screen roles with the ease of a gentle lady.

Following their postwar refits, the two queens were an enormous success for eleven years. Cunard, its emblem a lion holding the world in its paws, also carried the "lions share" of the North Atlantic passenger trade. Of this share, the giant sisters laid claim to a sizable portion. A one million peak was reached in 1957.

The *Mary* had lost the Blue Ribband (an award given for the fastest average speed in crossing the Atlantic) to the *United States* in July 1952. This liner beat the Queen by a comfortable margin with 35.59 knots, but

Such luxury was not available on the troopship.

her maximum speed was kept a secret. She had been built on warship lines, and it has since been revealed that she could have achieved forty knots.

The Cunard management became complacent with their ships making money hand over fist. They did not recognize the airplane as a serious threat to sea travel and they built up a large shore staff that administered from several offices in each country of operation. Money was being made, but it was also being spent almost recklessly.

In 1958, when the number of passengers by air equaled the number by sea - one million each - the problem stared Cunard in the face. It could no longer be ignored. By 1964, the figures showed that four million had traveled by air during the same period Cunards carrying capacity had fallen to 650,000. One particular voyage, November 1961, became typical of winter travel, with the *Mary* carrying just over 470 passengers out of her capacity of moe than 2,000. Crew members remained at the same level of more than 1,000.

To help reduce costs in 1963, the summer drydocking was omitted. These had always occurred during the *Queens* peak season, but by cutting the two annual overhauls to just one in the winter, Cunard gained revenue from an additional summer voyage and saved the cost of the peak-season lay up.

Our dining accommodations were slightly different.

Since fewer passengers were traveling during the winter months, Cunard decided to put the queens to cruising. For the *Mary* , this would mean the first cruise, in February 1963, that a Cunarder had made from Britain since 1939. During the ensuing years, she cruised from Southampton to Las Palmas and from New York to Nassau and the Mediterranean. Because of her size, she could not anchor in these ports (along with many more) nor could she could traverse the Suez or Panama Canals to reach further lucrative markets. Her lack of air-conditioning was also a great drawback.

By 1966, the *Mary* was still fast, still showing her fighting spirit, when she crossed the Atlantic at 29.68 knots. That same year saw the disastrous seamens strike that lasted for six weeks and cost Cunard nearly *f*4 million. Even though calls at Cobh were instigated in 1967, and there were new ports of call, and new itineraries for cruising, the *Queen* was now losing up to £ 8,000 a day.

In 1965, a new chairman had been appointed by Cunard, and his philosophy was intended to make the line pay, no matter how drastic or unpopular his proposals.

As a consequence, Captain William Laws opened a sealed envelope on board the *Queen Mary* on May 8, 1967. Contrary to what previous Cunard chairmen had said about the long-term viability of the queens, Sir Basil Smallpiece announced:

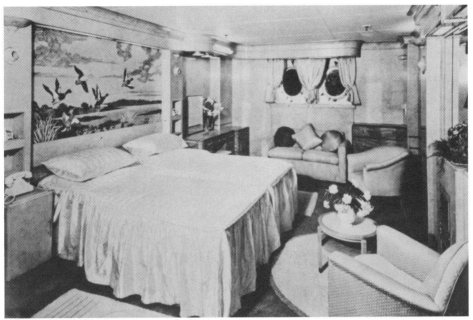

So were our sleeping accommodations.

"It is a matter of great regret to the company and to me personally, as it will be to friends about the world, that these two fine ships, the *Queen Mary* and the *Queen Elizabeth*, must shortly come to the end of their working lives. They hold a unique position in the history of the sea, and in the affections of seafaring people everywhere. But we cannot allow our affections or our sense of history to divert us from our aim of making Cunard a thriving company and no other decision will make commercial sense."

It was then decided to put the *Mary* up for sale. Cunard did not particularly want her to go to scrap, but neither did they want her to be operated in competition with them.

After receiving many bids, with many a strange suggestion being submitted, Cunard accepted a $3,450,000 offer from the City of Long Beach, California, the deal being signed August 18 by representatives of Cunard and the corporation of Long Beach. The ship would be used as a maritime museum, conference center, and hotel.

So, after years of memorable and faithful service, the *Queen Mary* was to be pensioned off. Her initial building cost of ƒ5 million had earned Cunard ƒ132 million. She had sailed just over 3,790,000 miles, had carried 2,114,000 passengers and had won herself an immortal place in the affections of a nation and in the seafaring annals of the world.

The *Mary* left New York on September 22, 1967, at noon amid momentous and tearful farewells. Despite a two-day storm, she arrived

A DC-9 dropping carnations on the deck of the Queen Mary, welcoming her to Long Beach. This was also done on her maiden voyage — by a DC-2.

at Southampton September 27, having achieved 27.86 knots on this, her 1001st crossing. She met a welcoming reception of fireboats, small craft, and a mostly silent crowd on shore. The mood was subdued.

Captain John Treasure Jones was the *Marys* master for her last Atlantic voyage, one of the most natural public-relations-oriented captains that Cunard has ever had. He had experienced a varied and interesting career with White Star - after less than fifteen years with this company, he was released following the amalgamation with Cunard. Stevedored in Liverpool; joined Cunard White Star; became a naval commander during the war after being torpedoed and commanding antisubmarine patrols; and, as a commander, became Divisional Sea Transport Officer in the Dutch East Indies. He rejoined Cunard after the war and joined the *Queen Mary* for the first time as chief officer in 1953.

"The one that I was currently captain of" was always his favorite ship. He became captain of the *Mary* during her last days at sea.

When he was asked by Cunard if he was surprised at the *Queen Marys* forthcoming disposal, John Treasure Jones replied, "No, Im not surprised. Im just surprised that youve kept her going for so long and losing so much money!"

During her ultimate crossing, the *Mary* met her younger sister, the ships "closing in" to within one mile of each other. At ten minutes past

Meeting-room facilities, Hotel Queen Mary.

midnight on September 25, the two largest liners passed each other on the dark Atlantic, brilliantly lit and with funnels floodlit, providing an unforgettable experience to the few who braved the lateness of the hour and the wind. This last poignant meeting was over in a few minutes as the liners sped by each other at a combined speed of 60 knots. Never again would they meet.

Everywhere the *Queen Mary* went there were crowds to see her arrive or depart. Ten thousand people watched the *Queen* sail from Southampton on Tuesday, October 31, 1967. The day before, the ports floating crane had lifted two red London buses onto the liner, where they were secured aft on the main deck. These buses would be used to transport tourists from downtown Long Beach to the ship once she had been located in her new home.

The City of Long Beach in Orange County, California, had bought the *Mary* and her value quoted on her export license was $3,450,000.

In the agreement, Cunard was to deliver the ship and to supply the minimal crew to do so and the fuel for a slow-speed voyage. But the new owners wanted the delivery trip to become a cruise, even though the ship did not have facilities for hot weather. She would also have to go via Cape Horn with its inherent dangers. So Long Beach arranged for Frugazy Travel to sell the trip as "The Last Great Cruise" in order to

The dining room and staff, Hotel Queen Mary.

recoup some of the $650,000 delivery costs. One thousand ninety-three passengers paid up to $9,000 each, and a profit of $125,000 was realized. Eight hundred six crew were taken on (119 deck, 98 engine and 589 catering staff), but they were overworked and only after intense negotiations was overtime paid.

Forty-seven hundred tons of fuel and 8,560 tons of fresh water for various purposes were loaded but this would have to be replenished enroute, as the *Queen Mary* had been designed for the Atlantic route and not for the 14,559-mile journey she was about to undertake. Seven stopovers had been arranged for the ship at ports that were capable of handling her.

HRH Queen Marys personal standard had been taken off the ship and stored safely until it could be installed on the new *QE2*.

So, at 9:30 a.m. on October 31, with pilot Jack Holt once more on the bridge, the Band of the Royal Marines playing "Auld Lang Syne" on the quayside, with fourteen naval helicopters flying in anchor formation overhead, and a "310" foot long pennant flying from her mainmast the *Queen Mary* left berth 107 in a tearful farewell. Workers in the city climbed on the roofs of their shops to witness her passing, and, as the *Mary* went by, the *Oriana* signalled, "Adieu, great *Queen*". The liner replied, "Thank you, thank you, thank you very much and good luck to you all."

Tears ran down the face of the *Queen Mary's* Master at Arms - "Oh! That was a grand, grand goodbye." Crowds waved and vessels blew their sirens as the *Mary* sailed by. Passing by Cowes for the last time, the *Mary* read a signal from the exclusive royal Yacht Squadron, "I am sorry to say goodbye. Very best wishes."

The passage to Lisbon, her first port of call, was rough and took about two days. In the English Channel enroute she passed HMS *Hermes*, the British aircraft carrier whose company lined the flight deck to cheer the *Queen* rousingly.

The *Queen* had to make a slow passage (which chagrined many a misunderstanding passenger) of around 20 knots. This was done to conserve fuel; she would use 1,100 tons on the North Atlantic to maintain her high speed, but this would consume the fuel too quickly, so only two engines and half the boilers were operational. As a result, only 550 tons of fuel were burnt daily. The journey to Rio de Janeiro from Las Palmas would cover 3,540 miles, and once there, the *Queen* was again refueled with 2,460 tons.

Early on the morning of her arrival in Rio, on Monday, November 13, a heat stroke caused the death of fish cook Leonard Horsburgh, aged 56, who had been known as "Lobster" to his friends because of his ruddy complexion. Once again the lack of air-conditioning could be blamed for a death aboard the ship. Maybe it was fitting that even on this last trip, the lack of air-conditioning should take its toll.

By the time of the ship's arrival at Rio, the "Mermaid Bar" had been reduced to using paper cups, through pilferage of glasses for souvenirs, and had become known as the Lily-Cup Bar. In port, funds had been raised among the crew for one of them to go ashore to buy liquor for use on board. When the time came for the *Mary* to sail the assignment had not arrived and the purchaser was beginning to feel that he might become none too popular.

As the ship sailed, a tug raced out of Rio and the *Mary* slowed; a cargo port was opened and various boxes were taken on board. These were detailed as Ship's stores, but they were, in fact, the belated packages of "crews" booze!

The burial at sea of Len Horsburgh took place at 11:15 a.m., and his body was committed to the deep. The captain had in all good faith chosen this relatively late hour for the commitment to show the passengers what a burial at sea was like. The passengers treated the event as an additional spectacle not on the published itinerary, and the crew members were upset when cameras clicked during the burial.

It became increasingly difficult to maintain communications between

Cunard in England and the captain of the ship heading south. Frequently, long delays occurred. Finally, Cunard radioed Captain Treasure Jones, "Get her there by yourself and don't try to contact us," and he was thus given the ultimate authority to handle the ship on his own. The captain was delighted; he welcomed and enjoyed the responsibilities thrust upon him and said later that being in sole charge of the *Mary* was like having "....a wonderful and beautiful toy that you have to be very careful with!"

On Sunday, November 19, the *Queen* passed Cape Horn in mid-afternoon. No one knew what the weather was going to be like, but it turned out to be cloudy and clear, with a moderate northeast wind creating a slight swell. For four hours, people lined up to pay $1 to ride on a London bus around the Horn. The proceeds went to an orphanage in Valparaiso, Chile, and certificates were given out to mark the "rounding". One man dove into the swimming pool to say that he had swum around the Horn while another pedaled away on a bicycle in the gym! That night, the weather took a turn for the worse just to show what the Horn could really offer.

The rest of the journey up the west coast of South America toward Valparaiso continued to be rough, and she arrived at the port on November 23, having completed the longest part of her journey, 3,895 miles. The next stopover was at the old sailing ship port of Callao on the 28th, and then Balboa, where fuel was taken on.

On December 5, she arrived and stayed overnight in Acapulco. All the crew had shore leave (save for safety parties), and, for a change, the *Queen* was feted. Champagne cocktail parties had been held since Valparaiso, with caviar and Havana cigars being rather freely distributed. This was due not so much as to the party spirit prevailing on board but to U.S. import restrictions on foodstuffs and a ban on Cuban imports.

A DC-9 jet, 500 miles from Long Beach, met the *Queen* and, repeating an incident that occurred on her maiden voyage in New York, bombarded the liner with flowers, most of which missed. However, the airliner's captain, A. Heimerdinger, later sent Captain Treasure Jones a framed and signed photograph of the event.

The arrival at Long Beach was nothing short of spectacular, as "Eight thousand if there was one!" boats came to meet the ship fifteen miles out in order to escort her to her berth. The *Queen*, once again, as on her maiden voyage to New York, received a royal welcome. The craft kept well clear of the liner, as her course had been well publicized by the authorities. Her sea lane was made into a federal waterway, with a year's imprisonment or a $2,000 fine for those who infringed it.

By 11:30 a.m. Saturday, December 9, 1967, amid the noise and cheering of an estimated million people, the ship came alongside her berth. The *Queen* had completed her last voyage. At 2:50 p.m. the passengers began to disembark, and at 4 p.m. two stowaways were landed into the care of the FBI. At a brief dockside ceremony, the captain was presented with a flowered key to the city, and he handed over the Cunard house flag. The crew were flown home almost immediately, as their 72-hour visas would not allow them much time for sightseeing.

On the following Monday, a slightly delayed ceremony took place on board, aft of the Verandah Grill. A telephone linked the ship with Cunard in London, and Lord Mancroft informed Captain Treasure Jones that the "...Long Beach cheque was a good one and had not bounced!" As the American flag was raised to take the place of the British ensign, the captain felt a lump in his throat, realizing that it was all over.

So ended the long and eventful sailing career of the Royal Mail Ship *Queen Mary*. She was to become a hotel, after a planned $8 million (later raised slightly to $100 million plus) conversion. She is now known as the Hotel *Queen Mary* and advertised as "81,000 tons of fun!" She has since been joined by Howard Hughes' giant flying boat, the *Spruce Goose*, and has also changed hands, with her ownership passing to the Wrather Corporation.

But she still remains a monument to the ingenuity and craft of British shipbuilding, a memorial to thousands of soldiers who traveled in her during time of war and a symbol of peace between two great nations that have so much in common.

The *Queen* is still remembered and her memory cherished. To mark the occasion of the 50th anniversary of her maiden voyage, her grand descendant the *Queen Elizabeth 2* undertook a "Queen Mary Anniversary Voyage" from Southampton on Saturday, May 3, 1986. The Queen Mother enjoyed lunch on board the liner and met many of the *Queen Mary's* passengers and crew who had been on board for the maiden voyage.

As one of the GIs who sailed on this ship during the war, I would add my small voice in thanks for delivering me safely over there, and also for being a minute part of the history of this great ship. The Royal Mail Ship *Queen Mary* was now the Hotel *Queen Mary*, a far better fate than the *Normandie* that burned at the dock in New York and the *Queen Elizabeth* that burned in Hong Kong. As a retired hotelman, I feel that the change from sea duty to being a year-round hotel in Long Beach, California, is a fitting, genteel retirement for the *Queen*.

Appendix B

Meritorious Service Unit Plaque 149th Armored Signal Company

During the period 1 March–30 April 1945 the 149th Armored Signal Company fulfilled its mission, that of installation, operation, and maintenance of signal communication for the 9th Armored Division, in a most exemplary manner.

At the time of the exploitation of the Remagen Bridgehead, the communication problem confronting the 149th Armored Signal Company was of an extremely complicated nature. It was imperative to maintain communication between the bridge site and higher headquarters in order to control the huge flow of personnel, vehicles, and material across the only existing Rhine bridge. This was accomplished by the installation of a 100-mile telephone network, and supplementing this with a special radio net. Maintenance of the wire net was exceptionally difficult due to artillery, small-arms, and anti-aircraft fire, and due to excessive breakage by vehicular traffic.

In the rapid advance to the Mulde River, during the period 24 March to 30 April, the type of operation precluded extensive wire network, and placed the main emphasis on radio. Continuous radio communication was maintained over poor terrain and through intense interference. Many improvisations were necessary to insure this, and captured enemy equipment was utilized to the maximum.

The flow of signal supplies for the Division was maintained over badly stretched supply lines, often as long as 250 miles, and at no time was there a critical shortage of any item of signal equipment.

The record of service rendered by the 149th Armored Signal Company was made possible only by the tireless energy and unceasing devotion to duty of all personnel, and by their utter disregard for personal comfort and safety. The work of the 149th Armored Signal Company was accomplished under trying and hazardous conditions, and its performance reflects great credit upon all personnel and the military service.

Honorable Discharge

This is to certify that

GEORGE E MC AVOY 11 122 453 TECHNICIAN FOURTH GRADE

149th Armored Signal Company

Army of the United States

is hereby Honorably Discharged from the military service of the United States of America.

This certificate is awarded as a testimonial of Honest and Faithful Service to this country.

Given at   Separation Center
Fort Devens Mass

Date   9 January 1946

C W OATLEY
Major AGD

Appendix C

ENLISTED RECORD AND REPORT OF SEPARATION
HONORABLE DISCHARGE

1. LAST NAME - FIRST NAME - MIDDLE INITIAL	2. ARMY SERIAL NO.	3. GRADE	4. ARM OR SERVICE	5. COMPONENT
MC AVOY GEORGE E	11 122 453	Tec 4	Sig C	AUS

6. ORGANIZATION	7. DATE OF SEPARATION	8. PLACE OF SEPARATION
149th Armd Sig Co	9 Jan 46	Separation Center Ft Devens Mass

9. PERMANENT ADDRESS FOR MAILING PURPOSES	10. DATE OF BIRTH	11. PLACE OF BIRTH
41 Farwell St Lewiston Me	19 Jul 20	Arlington N J

12. ADDRESS FROM WHICH EMPLOYMENT WILL BE SOUGHT	13. COLOR EYES	14. COLOR HAIR	15. HEIGHT	16. WEIGHT	17. NO. DEPEND.
See 9	Hazel	Brown	5' 5½"	149 LBS.	2

18. RACE	19. MARITAL STATUS	20. U.S. CITIZEN	21. CIVILIAN OCCUPATION AND NO.
WHITE X NEGRO OTHER (specify)	SINGLE X MARRIED OTHER (specify)	YES X NO	Room Clerk 1-07.60

MILITARY HISTORY

22. DATE OF INDUCTION	23. DATE OF ENLISTMENT	24. DATE OF ENTRY INTO ACTIVE SERVICE	25. PLACE OF ENTRY INTO SERVICE
	1 Dec 42	1 Dec 42	Portland Me

SELECTIVE SERVICE DATA	26. REGISTERED YES NO X	27. LOCAL S.S. BOARD NO. None	28. COUNTY AND STATE None	29. HOME ADDRESS AT TIME OF ENTRY INTO SERVICE See 9

30. MILITARY OCCUPATIONAL SPECIALTY AND NO.	31. MILITARY QUALIFICATION AND DATE (i.e., infantry, aviation and marksmanship badges, etc.)
Radio Op 740	Marksman Rifle and Carbine Expert Gunner

32. BATTLES AND CAMPAIGNS

Rhineland Ardennes   Central Europe

33. DECORATIONS AND CITATIONS

Good Conduct Medal   American Theater Campaign Ribbon   Victory Medal
European African Middle Eastern Theater Campaign Ribbon

34. WOUNDS RECEIVED IN ACTION

None

35. LATEST IMMUNIZATION DATES				36. SERVICE OUTSIDE CONTINENTAL U.S. AND RETURN		
SMALLPOX	TYPHOID	TETANUS	OTHER (specify)	DATE OF DEPARTURE	DESTINATION	DATE OF ARRIVAL
10 Nov 43	10 Sep 45	8 May 45	Ty 23 Nov 45	20 Aug 44	ETO	26 Aug 44
				27 Dec 45	U S	3 Jan 46

37. TOTAL LENGTH OF SERVICE						38. HIGHEST GRADE HELD
CONTINENTAL SERVICE			FOREIGN SERVICE			
YEARS	MONTHS	DAYS	YEARS	MONTHS	DAYS	Tec 4
1	8	15	1	4	24	

39. PRIOR SERVICE	
None	ACT OF 194., AS AMENDED, TO ... ...ERSON TO WHOM THIS DISCHARGE WAS ISSUED. ADMINISTRATOR OF VETERANS AFFAIRS

40. REASON AND AUTHORITY FOR SEPARATION

Convn of the Gov't AR 615-365 RR 1-1 Demobilization

41. SERVICE SCHOOLS ATTENDED	42. EDUCATION (Years)		
None	Grammar 8	High School 4	College 0

PAY DATA

43. LONGEVITY FOR PAY PURPOSES			44. MUSTERING OUT PAY		45. SOLDIER DEPOSITS	46. TRAVEL PAY	47. TOTAL AMOUNT, NAME OF DISBURSING OFFICER
YEARS 3	MONTHS 1	DAYS 9	TOTAL $300	THIS PAYMENT $100	None	$7.50	$15.53 Vou Jan 46

INSURANCE NOTICE

E A NYQUIST   Major FD

IMPORTANT IF PREMIUM IS NOT PAID WHEN DUE OR WITHIN THIRTY-ONE DAYS THEREAFTER, INSURANCE WILL LAPSE. MAKE CHECKS OR MONEY ORDERS PAYABLE TO THE TREASURER OF THE U. S. AND FORWARD TO COLLECTIONS SUBDIVISION, VETERANS ADMINISTRATION, WASHINGTON 25, D. C.

48. KIND OF INSURANCE			49. HOW PAID			50. Effective Date of Allotment Discontinuance	51. Date of Next Premium Due (One month after 50)	52. PREMIUM DUE EACH MONTH	53. INTENTION OF VETERAN TO	
Nat. Serv. X	U.S. Govt.	None	Allotment X	Direct to V. A.		31 Dec 45	31 Jan 46	$ 6.60	Continue X	Continue Only	Discontinue

54. [fingerprint]

55. REMARKS (This space for completion of above items or entry of other items specified in W. D. Directives)

Issued Lapel Button
ASR Score 2 Sep 45   61

56. SIGNATURE OF PERSON BEING SEPARATED	57. PERSONNEL OFFICER (Type name, grade and organization - signature)
George E. McAvoy	JOHN W BATCHELDER 1st Lt CWS

WD AGO FORM 53-55
1 November 1944

This form supersedes all previous editions of WD AGO Forms 53 and 55 for enlisted persons entitled to an Honorable Discharge, which will not be used after receipt of this revision.

Appendix D

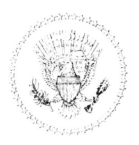

GEORGE E MC AVOY

To you who answered the call of your country and served in its Armed Forces to bring about the total defeat of the enemy, I extend the heartfelt thanks of a grateful Nation. As one of the Nation's finest, you undertook the most severe task one can be called upon to perform. Because you demonstrated the fortitude, resourcefulness and calm judgment necessary to carry out that task, we now look to you for leadership and example in further exalting our country in peace.

Harry Truman

THE WHITE HOUSE

Appendix E

Address by Major General John W. Leonard, Commanding General, 9th Armored Division, to Members of the 9th Armored Division, July 15, 1945

This is our third birthday. The 9th Armored Division, activated at Fort Riley, Kansas, July 15, 1942, with the mission of destroying the enemy, has done its full share in the accomplishment of this mission in the European Theater of Operations.

The Ardennes found us at St. Vith — in front of and inside Bastogne — and on the hinge in Luxembourg.

In the advance from the Roer River, we established a bridgehead over the Ahr River and at the same time electrified the world by seizing the Remagen bridge and winning the first bridgehead over the Rhine. This daring achievement shortened the war and saved many lives.

First to break out of the bridgehead, we seized Limburg, advanced to Warburg, and helped to complete the encirclement of the Ruhr.

Advancing to the Mulde River, we bypassed Leipzig and aided in its capture. In the words of the Commanding General, V Corps, "The 9th Armored Division gave numerous conclusive manifestations that the gallant men of which it is composed have mastered the art of armored warfare."

V-E day found the division in the vicinity of Karlsbad, Czechoslovakia, and Weiden, Germany. Today finds us performing our mission with the same thoroughness with which we destroyed the enemy. We will always give our best on any duty assigned to us.

Let each of us pause for a moment and in his own way pay tribute to those men of ours who have given their lives for their country. To their loved ones, we extend our sincere sympathy.

To our wounded, we extend our best and earnest wishes for their speedy recovery and their happiness.

My pride in you is honest, sincere, and humble. That God may bless each of you is my fervent prayer.

Index

The author in 1943.

About the Author

George Edward McAvoy was born at Lake Hopatcong, New Jersey, on July 19, 1920. He was educated in the New York City school system and moved to Maine in 1940. He entered military service from Lewiston, Maine, but had been working in the hotel industry for the Acheson Hotels up until that time.

McAvoy has written a history of the hotels around Mount Washington, New Hampshire, a book that also includes some history of New Hampshire's North Country. He was actively engaged in the hotel business in Maine and New Hampshire: as manager of the Littleton Hotel and co-manager of the DeWitt Hotel in Lewiston, Maine, and as proprietor, with his wife, of Thayers Hotel in Littleton, New Hampshire, co-owner of the Crawford House in Crawford Notch, and general manager of the Mount Washington Hotel at Bretton Woods for one season.

He spent six years as an administrative assistant to New Hampshire Governor Meldrim Thomson, Jr., holding the positions of Coordinator of Federal Funds, Director of Comprehensive Planning, Director of the State Civil Defense Agency, and Commissioner of the Office of Manpower Affairs. He also was the governor's alternate to the Federal Regional Council, the New England Governors' Conference, and the New England River Basin's Commission, and he held limited power of attorney in the Office of the Governor. He has also been chairman of the New Hampshire Historic Preservation Commission and a commissioner of the Human Rights Commission.

McAvoy has been active on local, state, and federal issues, as has his wife, Rita. Rita McAvoy received an appointment as assay commissioner of the U.S. Mint from President Richard Nixon and also was named to the Conservation Committee of the Department of Defense. She was reappointed to this commission by President Gerald Ford. They have two children, Richard Dixon, who is manager of the Ausable Club in St. Huberts, New York, and Suzanne Hopgood Lord, who is president of a financial consulting firm, The Hopgood Group, in Hartford, Connecticut.

McAvoy is an honorary member of the New Hampshire Hospitality Association, life and charter member of the Littleton Lodge of Elks, organizer and past director of the Peoples National Bank of Littleton, past president of the Littleton Rotary Club, past president of the Littleton

Chamber of Commerce, and organizer and past president of the Littleton Industrial Development Corporation. He holds office in degrees of the Masons and in September 1990 was elected a 33rd-degree Mason in Milwaukee, Wisconsin.

He has received the Public Service Award of the Federal Highway Commission, Department of Transportation, and the Distinguished Service Citation, DCPA, of the Department of Defense.

He entered the service on December 1, 1942, and was immediately assigned to the 9th Armored Division in Fort Riley, Kansas. He served with the 2nd Armored Signal Company (later named the 149th Armored Signal Company) as a radio operator and attained the rank of Technician Fourth Grade (Sergeant).